LIVING
WITH
HONOUR
WHAT'S EASY TO SEE IS EASY TO MISS

LIVING
WITH
HONOUR

WHAT'S EASY TO SEE IS EASY TO MISS

SHIV KHERA

MACMILLAN

© *Shiv Khera, 2003*

First Published, 2003

MACMILLAN INDIA LTD.
Delhi Chennai Jaipur Mumbai Patna Bangalore
Bhopal Chandigarh Coimbatore Cuttack Guwahati Hubli
Hyderabad Lucknow Madurai Nagpur Pune Raipur
Siliguri Thiruvananthapuram Visakhapatnam

Companies and representatives throughout the world

ISBN 1403 91102 9

Published by Rajiv Beri for Macmillan India Ltd.
2/10 Ansari Road, Daryaganj, New Delhi 110 002

Printed at Replika Press Pvt. Ltd., Kundli 131 028

To my mother for being my north star.
To my wife who is my true life partner.
To my children who are a blessing to me from God.

PREFACE

If you got all the wealth in the world and lose the soul – is it worth having?

This book is about living with honour – just what the title says.

What's easy to see is easy to miss too. Before looking for answers, we need to ascertain that we have the right questions. The greatest ignorance is·not to be aware of one's ignorance. Such ignorance cannot pass as innocence. People may suffer from inaction. Responsibility and prompt action go together. The objective of taking a courageous stand is to resolve challenges rather than prolong indecisions.

What Kind of Book is This

In a sense, this book is a road map. It describes the tools you will need for honourable living and offers direction for living with pride. It illustrates analyser that helps you find direction in a cluttered environment.

How to Read This Book

This book will help clarify issues that concern us on a day-to-day basis. Identify values, which not only help decision-making easier but make decisions that would give direction to the coming generations.

Please do not rush through this book. Go slow. Think through every page. Step back and think with the acquired knowledge – if you could roll back the clock, would you have taken the same decisions that you did in the past? Make notes on the side, highlight and mark that appeal to you the most.

Discuss these concepts with someone who is close to you.

Start an Action Plan

An idea dies unless it acted upon. The quiet knowledge if you don't use, you lose. The objective of this book is to help create an action plan to live with honour.

The principles in this book cut across Country, Culture, Religion. Throughout the book I have used masculine gender, only for the purpose of ease in writing. The principles in this book are universal.

ACKNOWLEDGEMENTS

Any accomplishment requires the effort of many people and this work is not different. I thank my daughters and especially my wife, whose patience and support was instrumental in accomplishing this task. I thank my staff whose diligent effort made this publication possible.

Many examples, stories, anecdotes are the result of a collection from various sources, such as newspapers, magazines, other speakers, and seminar participants, over the last 25 years. Unfortunately, sources were not always noted or available; hence, it became impractical to provide an accurate acknowledgement. Regardless of the source, I wish to express my gratitude to those who may have contributed to this work, even though anonymously.

Every effort has been made to give credit where it is due for the material contained herein. If inadvertently we have omitted giving credit, future publications will give due credit to those that are brought to the author's attention.

CONTENTS

LET'S GET STARTED!

There was a young executive who came home one day with a bag full of work. His five-year-old son wanted to play with him but the father said, "Son, I've got a lot of work to do, I'm behind in my office." The son said, "Dad, when I am behind in school they put me in a slower group. Why don't they put you in a slower group?" The father replied, "No Son, it doesn't work that way in the corporate world." But the child didn't understand. He still wanted to play.

The father finally thought of a way to keep the child occupied so that he could get on with his work. He had a magazine with a picture of the world on the cover. He pulled out the page and tore it into a number of small pieces, called his son and said, "Son, go put this picture of the world together and when you are done I'll come and play." He knew that it would take several hours. But within five minutes his son came back and said, "Dad, I am done." The man couldn't believe it till he saw it was all done. He asked, "Son, how did you do it? I need to learn from you." The son replied, "Dad, it was easy. On the other side of the picture of the world, was the picture of a man. All I did was to put the man together and turn it the other way round and the world came together."

You too can put the man together and the world will come together.

*H*onourable living is about accomplishment not just achievement. Honour and honourable living has many dimensions. It relates to individual, professional and social. All these dimensions are interconnected and influence one another. Weakness in any area could disrupt living with respect and dignity. A society is nothing but a composite of individuals. The collective behaviour of individuals is called culture. Some cultures are more conducive to honourable living than others. In those cultures, trust and transparency lead to general well-being of people.

Generally, culture influences individual behaviour.

Occasionally a strong individual emerges from the same culture and changes the direction of that culture for eternity.

In order to live with honour, we need to define the two words:

- Honour – is to live with dignity
- Honourable – is to be worthy of respect

Honourable living involves a sense of human dignity. In order to live with dignity we need to have a sense of:

1. Fairness – leads to justice
2. Empathy – leads to compassion
3. Integrity – leads to trust

The above three elements only come into play when there is vision in society. A visionary person must come up from within to bring and keep the society on track.

The biggest advantage of honourable living is that it gives meaning to life. A person feels complete, fulfilled and gratified which is the ultimate objective of an honourable person.

Come, let's walk together – to live with honour.

1

PRINCIPLES OF HONOUR

Ideas and Ideals

A young accountant was once offered a large sum of easy money for a job that made him somewhat uneasy. It wasn't quite illegal but struck him as unethical. He was confused whether he should undertake the job or not. He requested the client to give him a day to decide. That night, he went home and told his mother about the terms and conditions of the contract and the big money that was involved. His mother was totally an illiterate. After listening to him for two hours she said, "Son, I don't understand anything of what you just said. All I can say is one thing – that every morning when I come into your room, I find you fast asleep. I have a very hard time waking you up. I would hate to walk into your room one day and find you awake. The final decision is yours. You decide." With these words the mother left the room. The young man said to himself, "I got my answer."

*V*alues are intrinsic to our lives. They add to the strength of our character and the righteousness of our beliefs. All of us are entrusted with the duty of being promoters and protectors of values.

Values are Universal and Eternal

Truths don't change with time and calendar.

Through generations, some values have crystalised as eternal and universal which give us our clear "do's and don'ts". Today's concept of relative values says, "Everything is OK. What's right for me, may not be right for you." If values are subjective and they keep changing from person to person and situation to situation, then they are not values at all. In science, we look for theories and laws. In the commercial world, we look for guiding principles. Why, then, should we not look for universal benchmarks for values?

Whatever business or profession we may be in,

unless we have clear quality standards and benchmarks, how can we ever achieve them? Similarly, unless we have universal benchmarks for values and ethics how can we ever meet them? The question is, how do we set those universal benchmarks? I heard the following story which clarifies the point.

There was a frail, elderly woman, with two bags of groceries in her hand, waiting for a bus. Right behind her was a big boy, also waiting for a bus. The bus came. They both got in. It was packed. There was only one seat vacant at the far end of the bus and the lady started moving towards it. The big boy came from behind, threw his big arm around the lady, took one big step, and then another, and took that seat. The elderly lady fell on a few people's lap, all her bags of groceries got scattered and she was lying on the floor. There were many passengers in the bus. One of them was a sophisticated lady who thought, "How clumsy of this boy!" She was looking at the boy's etiquette and his manners. Another was a lawyer, who thought, "There must be a law against this kind of behaviour." He was looking at the legal aspect. A surgeon, also in the bus, thought, "This lady must have broken three ribs." He was looking at it from a surgical point of view. A fourth person in the bus was a psychiatrist who wondered if this boy was psychotic and needed mental help. Each of these four people were looking at the incident from four different viewpoints. One looked at social etiquette, others from legal, medical and psychological.

Not one of them raised the question, "Was this behaviour right or wrong?" Why don't we ask ourselves this question? The moment we do, we become judgemental. Why do we shirk being judgemental? If our value system is clear, what is wrong in being judgemental?

In order to establish universal benchmarks for values, we need to consider the following questions.

> One: Should the boy have behaved like this with the lady?
>
> Two: Should anyone behave like this with anybody at all?

If the answer to both questions is 'No'–you have found your universal benchmark. The same principle applies to all areas of our life.

In order to live our lives by worthwhile values, we need to be able to differentiate between right and wrong. This is not the kind of understanding that any of us is born with. It is something that we learn as we go along. Institutions like family, school, neighbourhood help form values. In turn, our values act as a binding force for our families and societies. They help a child become a good adult, go on to become a good spouse and a good parent. Strong values lead to strong families, which in turn prove to be an asset to society.

Peter Kreeft, a Professor at Boston College, in his book, *Making Choices*, writes that contrary to popular belief, there are some clear values. Once, just to prove his point, he made a statement in his class, "All women in my class flunk." Immediately everyone protested, "Not fair!" So, he asked them, "Who defines fairness?" If fairness is subjective, then there can be no universal values. The students then would have no right to impose their values on their teacher and neither the teacher on the students. But if there existed universal objective values called justice and fairness, then he would be judged wrong. And if there were no such thing, then all that the students could do was to protest against his rule because their subjective standards were different from his.

In this example, the question was not of liking or not liking the rule, but of fairness. What makes acts like murder, rape, torture and oppression crimes? The fact is that they fail the universal benchmark of fairness and justice. Whenever we think and talk of values, we need to ask, "Whose values are we talking about?" and "Who are we to judge?" We are talking about universal and eternal values, which cut across country, culture and religion. Since we have to live with universal benchmarks, it flows naturally that we have to judge? Just as truth doesn't change with season, facts do not disappear just because they are ignored. The same holds true for good values. Unlike success which is fleeting, values endure.

Fleeting Values

We often hear people comment on the degradation

of values in society. How can we have degradation unless we have a grade? When we don't meet standards, there are two choices – either increase our efforts to meet the grade or lower the benchmarks. If we choose to lower the benchmarks, degradation seeps in. The question is – why would a person compromise to lower the standards? Because they accept degeneration as a way of life and think the pain is not worth the gain. The more we compromise on our values, the greater the degradation and damage we cause to our society. It is no wonder then, that over a period of time, the degradation of family, social and political system becomes acceptable to us.

When people don't have the right values, what do they do?

> ➤ They lie to their employees and employers.
> ➤ They lie to their customers and colleagues.
> ➤ They lie to their spouse and children.

When they come to work, they take your pens and pencils home, make personal calls at company time. Is that what they are getting paid for? If someone steals your wallet, what would you call that person? A thief! And when we do all these things, what are we?

A strong belief in values is our best defence against the erosion of our moral fibre. All of us in our everyday lives find ourselves in situations where our ethical standards are put to test. When faced with such situations, people with weak foundations end up compromising their values. This, in turn, lowers their self-esteem, making it easier for them to compromise the next time round. Personal values are not different from professional values. Virtue and vice, idleness and hard work, good and evil, integrity and hypocrisy do not go together. To restore pride in ourselves and enthusiasm for righteous living, we have to stop treating our values like commodities with a price tag. Protecting our values is both a process and a product.

Consistency

Consistency is value-based behaviour. Consistency does not mean repeating the same behaviour all the time. It means behaving in the same way under similar situations. Consistency leads to reliability. If under ten similar situations, a person behaves in ten different ways – he becomes unpredictable and in turn – unreliable. This is erratic behaviour and such a person cannot be trusted. Consistency in behaviour reflects one's sense of values. It helps us avoid confusion and comes from having carefully evaluated facts before arriving at a decision.

Character

Character is about honour. It is the sum total of many qualities which reflect values. It is about integrity, honesty, ethics, conscience, loyalty, mental toughness, courage and consistency. It is a composite of qualities, not a commodity.

Integrity

The integrity of a person is not measured by his status or profession but by his conduct. It demands a clear-cut distinction between right and wrong with no grey areas in between. It requires moral courage in the pursuit of an ideal. Integrity combined with enthusiasm and determination makes for honourable living.

A person with integrity is a one-man army.

Good leaders believe strongly in making integrity a way of life.

A braham Lincoln was a very successful practising attorney. Once someone asked him to take up a case. After hearing the details Lincoln said, "I understand your case. It's technically strong but ethically weak. I cannot accept it. Because while I am arguing it, at the back of my mind all the time, I'll keep saying to myself, 'Lincoln, you're a liar. Lincoln, you're a liar.' I will not be able to live with myself."

Lincoln's unsaid message is pretty clear: "I sell my professional time, but not my conscience." It's worth repeating, *"I sell my professional time, but not my conscience."* Integrity fosters a feeling of security and confidence. A pillow of clear conscience affords the soundest sleep, and comes from a life lived with integrity. When a person tries to get out of a difficult situation through dishonest or unjust means, he really multiplies his problems till he reaches a point of no return. One can prevent this from happening by practising integrity in one's daily life.

When a person compromises his values, he not only loses the respect of others, but most importantly, he loses respect for himself. The lack of integrity cannot be compensated by any other quality of body or mind. The greatest virtue that people look for in each other is integrity. *Test yourself by asking, "If the world were watching me, would I still act the way I do?"* The answer to that would bring clarity about your stand on values.

Practising integrity takes courage.

Wisdom and integrity combine to give us strength, which enables us to live honourably. Wisdom is that virtue, that faculty of the mind, which helps a good person to apply his ability to bring efforts to fruition. Knowledge displayed timely is wisdom. Wisdom flows from both the head and the heart. It gives direction to courage.

Abundance of Common Sense is Wisdom

Once a clerk refused to sign on a form certifying that the stock tallied with the amount without first checking it, because certification without inspection would have meant accepting responsibility. This angered his dishonest supervisor who was in a hurry to get the certification so that he could accept charge at another location. The store clerk was almost ready to sign. Even though, terrified of what his boss might do, something within him urged him not to sign without inspection because the supervisor had a reputation for being corrupt. Later, upon verifying stocks, it was discovered that over 50% of it was missing. If he had given in to the feeling of cowardice, he would have signed the papers and got into trouble later.

The clerk's behaviour was both ethical and wise but most of all it was courageous. His signature would have made him responsible for helping a corrupt official indulge in malpractice. Eventually, the matter came up before the top management and he was rewarded with a promotion for his courage and honesty.

Seeing and knowing what's right and still not doing it shows lack of conviction. The above example reinforces that mere desire to do the right thing is clearly not enough. We judge ourselves by our intentions whereas the world judges us by our actions.

The Bible says, "The path to hell is paved by good intentions."

Action must follow good intentions.

We imbibe values not as facts but rather from the lives of our parents and other role models. These early lessons stay with us and become powerful reminders and reference points for helping us live our lives well. As adults, the choices we make depend upon the values we have learned during our formative years. These give us a clear sense of direction and the ability to distinguish between right and wrong.

Honesty – or an Eyewash

A man lying on his deathbed promised God that if he stayed alive and got well he would sell his palatial house and give away the money to the poor. Miraculously, the sick man began to recover and eventually got well. He remembered his promise but could not bring himself to part with his house. So he devised a plan. He advertised to sell his house for only a token sum of one silver coin on the condition that anyone who bought the house would also buy his dog for a million dollars. Very soon, he found a buyer. He sold the house, put the million dollars in his pocket and gave the silver coin to charity.

Who are we kidding? The real test of honesty is carried out in the face of temptation. The man in the above story fulfilled the promise that he had made to God. Even though he kept his word, he violated its spirit. Often when our conscience tries to call us, the line is too busy.

What is the Difference between Integrity and Honesty?

Integrity is a core value, whereas honesty or dishonesty is a habit. People who constantly practise telling the truth, get caught the first time they tell a lie. Reverse it. People who constantly tell lies, get caught the first time they tell the truth. A person may be honest but could still be lacking integrity. A teacher once asked a student, "Son, if you found a wallet with a large amount of money, what would you do?" The student replied, "If no one was watching me, I would keep it." The teacher said, "Son, you are honest, but you lack integrity." The student has demonstrated his honesty by admitting to the teacher what he would do but his act of keeping the wallet that did not belong to him showed lack of integrity.

Converse is true as well. One could be dishonest in work yet maintain integrity. Sometimes when racial riots break out, mobs come looking for innocent people to kill. If you give shelter to them and lie – that's dishonest in words, but shows integrity to values. Would you rather be honest and have an innocent person killed? Is that integrity?

There are signs that read: "Honesty is the best policy!" Is it really? When honesty is used as a policy, it is corrupt. It is like a trump card you have up your sleeve: when you need it, you pull it out, otherwise, you push it back. When honesty is used to suit one's convenience, it no longer remains a virtue. To some, honesty becomes habitual.

Honesty and dishonesty are both learnt traits.

Honesty and dishonesty are not the monopoly of the prosperous or the poor. Either could be honest or dishonest. Dishonesty derives from poor self-esteem. Genuine honesty is motivated more by the desire to do the right thing than the desire to not get caught. It does not look for concealment. Some people believe honesty restricts them. In fact, it's the opposite that is usually true. Honesty frees people from lies and creates an environment where they can communicate openly, take risks and be creative.

Honesty is its Own Reward

A contractor, who had made a fortune building homes, told his supervisor of 35 years, "I'm going to build one last house and you will build it for me because I will be gone for a year. Use the best material – money is no consideration. Make it the greatest house we've ever built." Having given these instructions, the man left. The supervisor thought that this was a great opportunity to make a fortune. He used the cheapest material inside but made the house look beautiful on the outside. After a year, the contractor returned. He inspected the house and asked the supervisor what he thought of the house. The supervisor replied, "It's the best house I've ever built." The contractor handed over the deed to him and said, "This is my parting gift to you."

What is the moral of the above story?

➢ Always do the right thing, even if no one is watching you.

➢ Develop a high standard of personal ethics.

Whether he knew the house was coming to him or not is the mute point. The question is: Is practice of integrity situational?

Truth is a pre-condition to justice and trust. How can we have an honourable relationship in business, friendship or fidelity in marriage when we cannot trust one another? The answer is we cannot. Lack of commitment and truthfulness of vows impoverishes individual and society emotionally.

People of character are trustworthy and they value their reputation. They realise that they are neither perfect nor infallible. And they are not afraid of accepting their mistakes. People, who are not trustworthy, regardless of their other qualities, reflect insincerity. Trust cannot be demanded by force, or bought with money. It is earned and inculcated through honesty and integrity. Meeting people who have a clear conscience gives one a feeling of comfort and trust in them because honesty inspires trust. *Trust in many ways is a much greater compliment than love. Often, there are people in our lives whom we love but cannot trust.*

ACTION PLAN

Walk a little further for the action plan...

SELF-EVALUATION SHEET

_____

_____

_____

_____

_____

_____

_____

_____

_____

_____

_____

_____

_____

_____

_____

_____

_____

2

FOUNDATION FOR SUCCESS

Not-so-secret Ingredient

A surgeon is looking forward to his daughter's wedding, a once-in-a-lifetime event. The proud father, all dressed up, is welcoming the guests. Suddenly the phone rings. "Doctor, we have an accident victim here bleeding profusely. We tried to reach the other doctors in town but no one is available. If you don't get here immediately, he'll die." What does the bride's father do? The answer is, he goes. Does this mean he loves his daughter any less? Not at all.

When our value system is clear, decision-making becomes a lot easier even though they may not be easy decisions.

Ethics

Ethics is a commitment to a higher order of moral values and an ability to distinguish right from wrong. People who are ethical are scrupulously honest. Ethical people set standards in behaviour and maintain the trust and respect of those around them, sometimes even at their own expense. They never compromise their ethical standards for material gains.

Ethical behaviour can be compared to the air we breathe in. Air is crucial to our life on earth but we never pay any attention to it until we begin to have trouble breathing. Similarly, we tend to take ethical behaviour for granted until it's missing from our lives and we fall victims to unethical behaviour.

All of us should want to do the right thing. Doing what is right builds one's self-confidence.

Ethics, and how we practise them, give meaning to our lives. Clear values reflect ethical decisions. The easier decisions in life are between right and wrong. The tougher decisions are between what's right and what's more right. A choice between right and more right automatically makes more right as most appropriate and less right as inappropriate.

Conscience

There was a robber who amassed a lot of ill-gotten wealth. One day, he went to a teacher who had a reputation of great character and asked, "How can I attain happiness? I have lots of wealth and five hundred thieves ready to obey me but somehow I still feel incomplete and empty." The teacher led him to the base of a hill, and pointing to three large stones, asked the robber to carry them and follow him up the hill. The robber could hardly move and said, "I cannot follow you with this heavy burden." So the teacher asked the robber to drop one stone. After going a little distance, the robber found it impossible to go up the hill with the two heavy stones. The teacher asked him to drop one more and the same thing happened with the third one and then the robber was able to easily follow the teacher to the top of the hill. The teacher said, "Deviating from the path of righteousness does cause a heavy conscience. Just as you could not climb the hill with the burden of the heavy stones, you cannot achieve happiness if you go through life carrying a heavy conscience."

How true. Whenever we go against our values, our conscience gets burdened. Stress level goes up. Insecurity comes in. Ignoring conscience long enough kills it eventually making it dead weight like the rocks in the story. Life becomes a burden.

Conscience and Ethics Go Together

Ateacher gave an exam to her class. As she began to read the correct answers for the students to mark their answers, one of the examinees changed an answer further down in the paper. It occurred to him that the teacher might think he had changed an answer the teacher had just given. He raised his hand and asked the teacher what he should do about changing answers after the teacher had started reading the correct ones. The teacher replied, "Let your conscience be the guide."

Conscience is a direction prior to an action. It acts not just as a guide but also as a brake. It is a fence not just a path. Conscience is the guiding lamp that makes us do the right thing simply because it is the right thing to do, irrespective of personal ends.

The only tyrant I accept in this world is the still voice within.

– Mahatma Gandhi

Loyalty

There is an ancient tale from India. King Yudhisthir, a brave and just king, decided that he had spent enough time on the earth and was now ready for Heaven. His wife, Draupadi, and his four brothers accompanied him. A dog followed them faithfully. The journey was long and difficult, and by the time Yudhisthir arrived at the gates of Heaven, his wife and brothers had fallen by the way. He was invited to walk through the gates but Yudhisthir refused to enter Heaven without his family. Lord Indra then explained that his family had already arrived and awaited him inside. Yudhisthir was on the verge of accepting the invitation when he realised that the dog was not permitted to accompany him past the main gate. Yudhisthir was determined not to desert a living creature that had followed him with such loyalty. Lord Indra could not believe that Yudhisthir was refusing Heaven for a mere dog. When asked to explain his decision, Yudhisthir replied that he could not betray the faithful and loyal dog that had followed him all the way. The gods were pleased with his reply. As it turned out, it was no ordinary dog but 'Dharma' himself who had wanted to test Yudhisthir.

Loyalty Breeds Loyalty

Loyalty is the hallmark of strong character in the same way as a tree is as strong as its roots. Loyalty calls for readiness to sacrifice. It is the most important quality one looks for in one's family, spouse, friends, employers and employees. A sense of loyalty in all relationships generates a sense of belonging. Loyalty is an attitude as well as an action. It survives inconvenience and temptations.

Whom do we owe loyalty to? We owe loyalty to our values. Where the value system between an individual and the organisation does not coincide, one cannot work in the same organisation. Either we change our value system or we change our organisation. Not only that, where the value system does not coincide within the family, we cannot live together. Either we change our value system or we change our family. Individuals and organisations are perishable, whereas value-based codes of conduct are everlasting.

External Benchmarks

The *Ten Commandments*, are "commandments" and not "suggestions". Therefore, they set clear benchmarks on ethical behaviour. Some of the ten commandments are:

- Don't steal.
- Don't cheat.
- Don't give false witness.
- Respect your parents.

Their universal appeal means that they have been respected and taught through all cultures, civilisations and times of history.

Rationalisation

Some people think it is not really stealing if the theft would go unnoticed, or the other person has enough of it anyway. Taking things that don't belong to us without permission even with the intention of replacing them before being found out, is stealing. Justification for stealing comes from the attitude that others exist for exploitation and to serve you.

It is common practice that people take and keep things that do not belong to them and rationalise their behaviour.

Once at a grocery store, I purchased a packet of disposable razor, priced at $7.95. As I was passing through the cash counter, a clerk scanned the razor and the display read $11.95. Since I had carefully noted the price, I told the clerk that there was a mistake and that the price should be $7.95. He double-checked his record and said, "The correct price is $11.95." To resolve the issue, he called the manager who wanted to see where I had picked the razor from. After seeing where the razor was kept and had been tagged at $7.95, he verified his records and said that it was mistakenly put on the wrong rack. The correct price was $11.95. In spite of my offering to pay since it was their mistake, he decided to give it to me complimentary.

I thanked him and left. I narrated the incident at a social get-together and to my disappointment, the first reaction I got was, "Next time when I go to the store, I will take an item which is sitting on a higher-priced rack and put it on a lower-priced rack and possibly get away by not paying." Is that honourable?

Does this sound familiar?

To some people, possession implies ownership. *Just because I have it, it doesn't mean it's mine.* By the same token, keeping extra change given mistakenly by a cashier or not paying for a dish that the waiter forgot to put on the bill, seems justified.

A similar instance is of a young girl who told her friends that she got a pair of shorts for free because the clerk made a mistake due to oversight and did not charge for it. She did not feel any obligation to pay. Her thinking was, "It was his fault. His mistake was my gain."

Stealing is not only that you rob material goods, even the leaking of confidential information of the employer to a competitor is stealing.

False advertising is another form of stealing. Besides embezzlement, another example of stealing is the taking home of office supplies without the knowledge of the employer.

Doing personal work in company time is another kind of stealing. Similarly, not paying what is due to others in time is stealing.

Just because the culprit is not easily identified for stealing, it does not absolve him of his responsibility.

Allowing impressionable-age children to watch inappropriate movies robs them of their innocence — that's stealing.

If something is not earned, bought, gifted or inherited, it is not yours. Similarly, what is kept in trust needs to be returned because it's not yours. The difference between borrowing and stealing is that borrowing implies consent and knowledge of the owner and stealing does not.

Is this honourable living? Can we live with ourselves?

Mental Toughness

If one of your loved ones was sick, would you want a doctor with character, dedication, discipline, mental toughness to do his best, or would you want a doctor with equal qualification but lacking these qualities? Why a doctor? The same principles would apply to an attorney, a salesman, parent, teacher, manager and so on.

Nobody promised us an easy life. Life seems easy when the going is good. But, often, we have to perform our best when we are feeling our worst. The time to work even harder is when the chips are down and when you are sad, sick and hurting. That requires mental toughness. Mental toughness is the ability to see the long-term gains rather than be put off by short-term pain. Once you have cultivated such toughness, you have gained the winning edge. Shun Fujimoto, Olympic gold medallist, gymnast, who performed in 1976 with a broken leg said, *"The pain shot through me like a knife... but now I have a gold medal and the pain is gone."*

---

*Leaders face challenges. It takes mental toughness
to endure inner pain. You need to plan for the best,
be prepared for the worst, expect surprises but
continue to move forward anyway.*

Leave your comfort zone

Mental strength lies in the ability to consciously
place yourself in a vulnerable position, taking risks
and getting out of your comfort zone. The result is
that you change your status from being a spectator
to being a player. Mental toughness helps you make
the right decisions, even though they may not be
the most pleasant.

IF

*If you can keep your head when all about you
Are losing theirs and blaming it on you;
If you can trust yourself when all men doubt you,
But make allowance for their doubting too;
If you can wait and not be tired by waiting,
Or, being lied about, don't deal in lies,
Or, being hated, don't give way to hating,
And yet don't look too good, nor talk too wise;
If you can talk with crowds and keep your virtue,
Or, walk with kings – nor lose the common touch;
If neither foes nor loving friends can hurt you;
If all men count with you, but none too much;
If you can fill the unforgiving minute
With sixty seconds' worth of distance run –*

Yours is the Earth and everything that's in it,
And – which is more – you'll be a Man, my son!

– Rudyard Kipling

Channel fear in the right direction

Fear is a natural body reaction in the face of danger. Fear is like fire – under control it is useful, but uncontrolled, it can destroy. Constantly living in fear leads to the loss of purpose of life. Real and imaginary fears can percolate through our thinking process and damage our personality. Anxiety also comes naturally when we see things are not going well for ourselves or for our loved ones.

Such negative emotions may actually trigger positive reactions in our body which energise us and help us cope with the threat with either a fight or flight response. Regardless of the outcome, terrifying situations can be learning experiences that prepare us for the future.

If we give in mindlessly to fear, we lose even before we have begun. Soldiers are taught to expect fear to grip their hearts and are then trained to overcome it. It is the firmness of spirit that meets danger without fear.

Commitment to Honourable Conduct

- A Doctor takes the Hippocratic Oath.
- A Legislator takes an oath to uphold the Constitution and serve the people.

- A Judge takes an oath to uphold justice.
- A Lawyer pledges to a code of conduct.
- A Police Officer takes an oath to uphold the law.

The underlying values of each oath rests on a foundation of ethics and morality. The common thread of integrity and fair play runs through each of them. Only a fair person can deliver *justice*, which can be defined as *truth in action*. Implementing justice takes both courage and competence.

These are three traits we need to imbibe to live with honour:

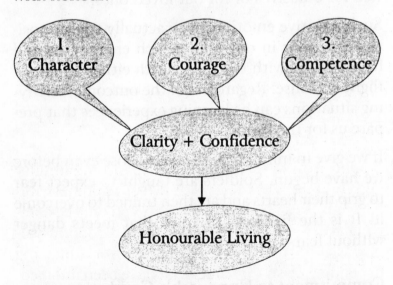

If any one of these three is missing, honourable living is endangered. What good is character, if we do not have the courage to implement it? And what good is courage, if we do not know what and how to implement it? And finally, what good is competence without the first two? Integrity and justice without courage is useless, just as courage without integrity and justice is oppression.

An honourable person is:

- Bold but not a bully
- Humble but not apologetic
- Confident but not conceited
- Proud but not arrogant
- Tender but not weak
- Strong but not rude
- Firm but not stubborn
- Cool but not cold
- In love with life but ready to die
- Content but not complacent
- Detached but not indifferent
- Wise but not otherwise.

Inculcating honesty, loyalty, compassion, humility and commitment in our lives brings happiness and harmony. Even love for our family can only be complete when we follow a well-defined code of values. A child can turn into a burden or a blessing depending upon the values that have been imbibed. Good character involves identifying, believing and practising good behaviour. Good behaviour stems from moral values which, through effort and practice, become ingrained in a person.

Build Me a Son

*B*uild me a son, O Lord, who will be strong enough to know when he is weak, and brave enough to face himself when he is afraid; one who will be proud and unbending in honest defeat, and humble and gentle in victory.

Build me a son whose wishbone will not be where his backbone should be; a son who will know thee, and that to know himself is the foundation stone of knowledge.

Lead him, I pray, not in the path of ease and comfort, but under stress and spur of difficulties and challenge. Here, let him learn to stand up in the storm; here let him learn compassion for those who fail.

Build me a son whose heart will be clear, whose goal will be high; a son who will master himself before he seeks to master other men: one who will learn to laugh yet never forget how to weep; one who will reach into the future, yet never forget the past.

And after all these things are his, add, I pray, enough of sense of humour, so that he may always be serious, yet never take himself too seriously. Give him humility, so that he may always remember the simplicity of true greatness, the open mind of wisdom, the meekness of true strength.

Then I, his father, will dare to whisper, "I have not lived in vain."

– Douglas MacArthur

ACTION PLAN

1. Identify three values that you would to want to live by:

   _____

   _____

   _____

2. Practise them consciously for 21 days in three areas of your life:

   (a) Family

   (b) Work

   (c) Society

3. Share these values with someone close to you in order to reinforce and crystalise your own values.

   The following steps can help you to create your own action plan at home and work:

- Setting a clear value-based code of model behaviour.
- Communicating the code to all concerned in absolute clarity.
- Ensuring that the ethical code is enforced.
- Recognise and reward ethical behaviour.
- Ensuring that short-term gains do not jeopardise long-term ethical objectives.
- Disciplining unethical conduct.
- Setting up role models.
- Developing a sense of pride in maintaining ethical standards.

SELF-EVALUATION SHEET

_____

_____

_____

_____

_____

_____

_____

_____

_____

_____

_____

_____

_____

_____

_____

_____

_____

SELF-EVALUATION
SHEET

3

GRACE UNDER FIRE

Firmness of Spirit

COURAGE FINDS ITS OWN WAY

Heaven never helps the man who will not act.

– Sophocles

There was an old farmer who in spite of having suffered many setbacks in his life always looked happy and cheerful. One day his friend asked, "How do you manage to keep your sense of humour in spite of such setbacks?" The farmer, with a sparkle in his eyes, said, "It is not difficult, you just need to learn to cooperate with the inevitable."

There is an old saying, "When nature throws a dagger at you there are only two ways to catch it, either by the blade or by the handle." Living with courage means to catch the dagger by the handle and use it as a tool to our advantage.

*C*ourage empowers. It is a tremendous tool when used constructively. Courage gives us the ability to be assertive and resist being paralysed. Lack of courage destroys our ability to act. We are turned into bodies that walk, talk and breathe but remain spiritually dead.

Courage is living by one's own values. It is moving forward with the belief that your actions are worthwhile. Courageous people always believe that something inside them is superior to their external circumstances. The difference between getting somewhere and reaching nowhere in life is courage. Courage demands taking risks, venturing into the unknown, facing obstacles, opposition, embarrassments and criticism with confidence.

The Many Dimensions of Courage

Courage to dream.	*Courage to face reality.*
Courage to show grace in victory.	*Courage to maintain honour in defeat.*

Courage to teach.	*Courage to learn.*
Courage to confront.	*Courage to be confronted.*
Courage to show anger.	*Courage to apologise.*
Courage of conviction.	*Courage to challenge our false convictions.*
Courage to speak out.	*Courage to listen.*
Courage to judge.	*Courage to forgive.*
Courage to love.	*Courage to face rejection.*

Small acts of courage gradually get strengthened to result in great acts of courage. C.Q., i.e. **courage quotient** has become equally important as I.Q. and E.Q. Endurance and bravery in the face of hostility are the hallmarks of courage.

One man with courage makes a majority.

– Andrew Jackson

What is *True* Courage?

Courage is another name for the ability to face criticism. It is easy to rationalise problematic behaviour. However, we need courage to challenge our self-limiting beliefs, face cynicism, false convictions, inflated egos and excuses.

It takes the courage of a soldier to live honourably. No matter what a person does, there will always be critics and the critics sometimes may be very convincing. True courage is what it takes to stand firm when you stand alone.

Abraham Lincoln demonstrated courageous leadership by signing the Emancipation Proclamation even when he faced lack of consensus.

True courage is also practising integrity and honesty with ourselves and with those around us. It is the ability to decide when to advance or retreat on the basis of our belief system. Beware of false courage that comes out of vanity. Real courage is demonstrated in behaviour and not words. The dangerous people are not the ones who openly disagree with you but the ones who disagree and are too cowardly to let you know. Moral courage is rooted in values and results in conviction.

Faith gives strength but doubts lead to weakness. Courageous people face trying situations with wisdom to preserve honour whereas cowards are inclined to take the crooked path.

There is a story from ancient times, about a mean moneylender, who had lent money to a trader. Because of setbacks one after the other, the trader was unable to pay.

The trader had a pretty young daughter and the devious moneylender had his eyes on her.

To show his devious helpfulness, he suggested that if the trader would agree to his marrying the young girl, he would forgive the debt or else hell would break loose.

Both the trader and the daughter were in a fix. The moneylender pretended to be generous by proposing that let fate decide. He proposed that he would put a black pebble and a white pebble into an empty bag and the girl would pick one pebble. And if she picked the black pebble, she would have to marry him and the father's debt would be forgiven. But if she chose the white pebble, she would not have to marry him and the debt would still be forgiven.

The daughter was not just pretty but also very intelligent. She didn't want her father to go to jail, she agreed to the proposition. The day came when the whole village collected to see the fate of the trader and his daughter. They were standing on the bank of the river full of pebbles.

The moneylender stooped down to pick up the two pebbles. Making sure nobody was noticing, he picked two black pebbles so that he could make sure he married the girl. Quietly, the sharp eyes of the girl were also watching. The girl was then asked to pick one pebble, upon which her and her father's fate rested. Supposing you were one of the spectators at this happening:

1. What would you have done?
2. What would you advise the girl to do?
3. How would you handle the situation?
4. What are the girl's choices?
   (a) She could expose the moneylender by asking him to show both the pebbles.
   (b) She could refuse and sacrifice her father.
   (c) She could take a black pebble and sacrifice herself to save her father.

The choices aren't easy. It was either her life or her father's life and she was not prepared to sacrifice anyone. And more so her father's.

Here is what the girl did.

She put her hand in the bag and picked one pebble knowing full well that they were both black. She was the only one who had seen what the moneylender had done. As she pulled her hand out of the bag, without looking at the pebble she on purpose lost her balance, fell on the ground and dropped the pebble. It got mixed up with others, so nobody could see what colour it was. She got up, apologised for her clumsiness and said, "Let's check what colour pebble is in the bag, that will tell us which one I picked." The pebble in the bag was of course black, it was assumed that the one she had picked was white.

In front of the whole village, the moneylender did not have the guts to accept his dishonesty. He had to live with his decision and both the father and the daughter went free. .

Her action was guided by the motivation to preserve honour. Her on-the-spot decision showed that wisdom is nothing more than timely application of common sense.

Those who love freedom are willing to accept the challenges of life so that they can live with respect and dignity.

Men of principles are bold but not all bold people are men of principles.

We often do things either to gain pleasure or to avoid pain. Moral cowards don't have the courage to pay the price to defend their beliefs. Courage lies not in accepting conditions blindly, but in daring to face the consequences.

The ability to believe in yourself when everyone has given up on you is a sign of courage. You know that you are vulnerable and yet you endure. Your faith in yourself helps turn dreams into reality. A great example in history is that of Galileo.

Galileo, at the age of 26, became a Professor of Mathematics at the University of Pisa. 400 years earlier people accepted all the ancient theories without questioning them, and the ancient Greek philosopher, Aristotle, was considered the greatest of all authorities. Questioning his theories was considered disrespectful. Galileo proved that weight has nothing to do with how fast objects fall. The rate of descent of an object depends on the resistance of air. This went against Aristotle's theory. Even though Galileo was able to demonstrate his theory, people chose not to believe him. They were afraid that discrediting one of Aristotle's principles may lead to his other principles being proved wrong too, and this made them feel threatened. No one came forward in support of Galileo but the great scientist did not lose faith in himself. He stood his ground, and in time, his theory met with both approval and acclaim.

Courage is the quality that enables a person to face adversity without succumbing to fear. Courage is neither fearlessness nor reckless behaviour. Courage is confronting fear. Recklessness often grows out of vanity and is foolish. The ability to choose the right thing to do requires wisdom. Courage is a demonstration of the wisdom to know when to take a firm stand.

Courageous behaviour inspires people and helps generate trust. Recklessness, on the other hand, can embarrass and even endanger people. It can lead to loss of trust. The courage displayed by Gandhi and Martin Luther King inspired others to stand against injustice non-violently even at the cost of great personal hardship. The movements they led achieved much for their followers, their countries and society as a whole.

Courage is a State of Mind

Strength and authority demonstrated by bullying or oppressing the innocent is not courage but cowardice. Bullying and oppression are a cover-up for insecurity. Courage does not flow from strength and authority, but is a state of mind. It can be cultivated but never faked. It is not a one time act but an automatic response. Courage empowers us to face life squarely, move forward and take charge.

"Courage may be the most important virtue because without it you won't have the strength to sustain any other value."

– Maya Angelou

The courage and ability to take decisions puts a person in the driver's seat. If you do not take control of your future, your future is automatically determined by other people's decisions. You have to move forward with the belief that your actions are worthwhile.

Human beings who lack courage and concern are a sad spectacle. People feel inadequate and lose their self-respect when they do not find in themselves the courage to respond to situations in life.

Endurance

Fortitude can be defined as a combination of patience and courage which enables a person to face adversity with calmness and grace.

Socrates was disgraced in his time as the immoral corrupter of youth and forced to consume poison when he refused to compromise on his beliefs.

His courage to stand by his beliefs, all alone, is what earned him the recognition of having been one of the greatest thinkers the world has known.

I was pleased with the 1988 Wimbledon because I pushed myself. At one point, I started getting a cramp in my foot, then my knee hurt. But I pushed myself anyway. I felt that I did my best. It was like, I was playing from within.

– John McEnroe

Courage to Face Reality

Refusing to acknowledge and accept reality is a habitual mindset for many of us. Denial can become a way of life if we are unwilling to accept constructive criticism. This is the philosophy behind the three monkeys who see no evil, hear no evil and speak no evil. Today, the philosophy has been changed to suit monkeys who see no truth, hear no truth and speak no truth. Facing reality can be upsetting and difficult, but if we do not cultivate the habit of being courageous, we may lose our own self-esteem and be trapped in a vicious cycle of failure.

Cowards die many times before their deaths.
The valiant never taste of death but once.

– William Shakespeare

Cowards are easily dissuaded. Some are more afraid of living than dying and look for security and not opportunity.

Courage is the power to overcome fear, danger, injustice and misfortune. Courage is that desire and ability which enables us to persist in spite of insecurities and intimidations. All fears percolate through our thinking process and damage our personality. By not practising courage, we deprive our loved ones as well as ourselves from living a purposeful and a meaningful life.

Players win, players lose, players prepare, players practise, players get hurt but players get up. No matter what the outcome is, players play.

*A*fter years of hard work, Thomas Carlyle finished the manuscript of his book *The French Revolution* and gave it to a friend to read. The friend's housekeeper mistook the manuscript for trash and threw it into the fire. When she got the news, Carlyle's wife could not hold back her tears. His friend stood trembling, and Carlyle himself was speechless. Finally, with a display of remarkable courage and restraint he said, "Accidents like these happen."

Although, outwardly Carlyle appeared courageous, he was devastated. He was unsure if he could continue with the project. He could not sleep all night. The next morning he resolved to start working on his book again. No matter what, he just could not give up. Two years later, he had recreated and finished his great work, *The French Revolution*, which remains to this day a living testimony to his indomitable spirit.

The greatest test of courage is accepting loss without losing heart. Challenges in life make or break us depending on the stuff we are made up of and the goals we want to achieve in life. The important thing is to know how to rise above the numerous disappointments that life has in store for most of us and achieve our goals despite disappointments.

The Sweet Music of Applause

As a child, Ludwig Beethoven could play the piano better than most adults. His father, a drunkard, was more interested in the money he could make using his son. But his mother was supportive. Ludwig was seventeen when she died leaving two younger brothers under his care. Young Beethoven soon grew to be recognised as a truly great musician. But misfortune struck when at the age of twenty-eight he became deaf. Deafness for a musician is especially cruel. But Beethoven overcame his disability with great courage and wrote some of his best music even after he had lost his ability to hear. At one time, Beethoven agreed to conduct an orchestra at Vienna. With his back towards the audience, he directed the music he himself could not hear. The audience was enthralled. When the recital was over, he kept standing with his back towards the audience, getting his things together. One of his companions understood what was happening and turned him around. Only then did Beethoven see that he was receiving a standing ovation. The audience, who saw that Beethoven could neither hear his own composition nor their standing ovation, were moved to tears by his exemplary courage.

Overcoming adversity takes exceptional inner strength as demonstrated by Beethoven.

Courage to Care

Marquis de Lafayette, a brave soldier of the American Revolution returned to his estates in France in 1782. He was a man known for his courage, integrity and idealism both in the United States and France. In 1783, though the wheat harvests in France were poor, Lafayette's barns were full. The foreman of his estate advised that he sell the wheat as prices were rocketing. To this Lafayette, knowing that the peasants of the surrounding villages were hungry, responded, "No, this is the time to give."

Caring comes from empathy. To a caring person, the honour of the other is just as important as his own. An honourable person does not put a price tag on humanity. To them, dignity is more important than financial gains.

Every act of love and care involves giving, and hence is an act of courage. To act courageously requires soul-searching and intelligence. Courageous action may not always bring happiness but there is no happiness without courageous action.

Courage to Dare

By the age of twenty-one, Copernicus was a learned man with extraordinary abilities. Popular belief at that time held that the earth was the centre of the universe and that the sun and the stars moved around it. The influential men then were the priests and the astrologers who gave their own interpretation of the heavens. Copernicus had the learning and the wisdom to see through the ignorance of the astrologers. He did his own study and found that the earth was not the centre of the universe but a small planet that revolved around the sun. His discoveries were not in tune with the times. Thus, he faced resistance from the Vatican, and the priests publicly denounced him. He was exiled and forbidden by the Church from speaking publicly on any matter that threatened the common belief as expounded by the Church. Secretly some people respected him and his work, but felt unsure about his sanity. Undaunted, Copernicus carried on writing about his new-found knowledge and after decades of effort he completed his work. Now, the insurmountable problem ahead of him was to get his findings published. Ever persistent, he went ahead and dedicated his book to Pope Paul III, a scholar, knowing fully well that only he would be capable of handling any opposition arising from the publication of his controversial book. In 1543, when Copernicus was on his deathbed, a messenger came and handed him a copy of his published book. Holding the book to his heart he breathed his last. Copernicus' courage and strength of conviction paid him rich dividends.

Popular beliefs may not always be right. They sometimes need to be challenged against all odds.

Courage Multiplies Your Ability

Whenever two people of equal ability compete, it is the more courageous of the two who wins. The courage you display can make the opponent wary and put him on the defensive.

Not tackling a problem head-on today, creates a

bigger one tomorrow. Tomorrow's problems may end up to be the results of today's short-sighted solution. Ignoring issues does not make the problem disappear but instead multiplies it. It makes sense to face short-term pain for greater gain in the future. It is not uncommon for a chest pain which is taken lightly in the beginning to lead to a severe heart attack later.

One individual with a backbone will accomplish more than a hundred men with a wishbone.

Courage is that firmness which confronts danger. It requires taking risks and seeking the unknown with a sense of responsibility towards oneself and those around.

Louis Braille was born in France about 200 years ago. His father made leather goods. One day, he hurt his eye while playing with an instrument used for stitching leather. The infe   spread to the other eye and he became totally blind. Blind people those days were treated with great cruelty, and their affliction was often seen as divine punishment. Louis' father sent him to a blind school where he met a retired soldier who taught him to read with the help of embossed dots. Braille started refining the script for the blind so that they could read by feeling with their fingers. By the age of twenty, Braille had conceived and published a book explaining how his system could be used by the blind for reading and writing. Braille not only overcame his own affliction but also helped blind people all over the world to empower themselves by reading and acquiring knowledge. Braille's method soon spread across the world. His story is an example of true courage in the face of the most trying circumstances!

People like Braille have enriched the world and are honoured till eternity.

Five Steps to Develop Courage

More important than what we get in life is what we become. Life is precious and priceless and so are we. When we change ourselves we also change the world around us. What we do and what we are, are inextricably linked in a dynamic cycle. As rational beings we can consciously change our thinking pattern and behaviour. The steps outlined below could help develop courage in us:

1. *Face up to reality*

Rationalisation is a psychological defence commonly used to avoid dealing with painful realities, and hence by default, accepting long-term pain. Refusing to acknowledge and accept reality becomes a mindset. When we don't see reality we start living in the past or in the future. We don't stop there. We distort reality and build up fears and doubts. We often worry about things that may never happen. Such imagined fears weaken a person.

2. *Re-examine your value system and take a stand*

Guidance may be sought from people who have a clear value system and the courage to take a stand. This is the guide that distinguishes courage from recklessness and stubbornness.

3. *Build character, build courage*

Character is the foundation that helps us confront our false beliefs and build courage. We need to review our core values and principles and resolve to be a person of integrity.

4. *Practise small acts of courage*

Courage is not like money in the bank. The more you spend it the more you get in return. We avoid the act of courage often for reasons of complacence and apathy than cowardice. We then become so comfortable with our discomfort that we start loving it. The trouble is that many of the problems we face today may have been solved more easily with a small courageous decision taken in the past.

5. *Perfect practice leads to preparation*

Prepare by trying to anticipate situations, and then be ready for the totally unexpected. Remember, practice does not make you perfect but makes permanent whatever you practise. Small choices in life end up becoming significant choices and prepare a person to face the bigger challenges of life.

Daily honourable living takes courage.

Weak people can never be sincere and cowards can never practise morality.

ACTION PLAN

How do we inculcate courage in our daily lives?

1. Ask yourself these questions:
    (a) How can I transform my life courageously?
    (b) What is it that I really want to do but never had the courage to do?
    (c) Which act of courage do I need to practise on a daily basis? What is of importance to me?

2. Make a list of your values, goals and dreams on an index card (three each).

3. Write down the outcome, the benefits you will get from achieving those dreams.

4. (a) Practise these three items daily (for minimum 21 days).

    (b) Accept responsibility for your actions and behaviour.

To live honourably, you need to enter into a contract with yourself and develop a profound relationship with life.

SELF-EVALUATION SHEET

_____

_____

_____

_____

_____

_____

_____

_____

_____

_____

_____

_____

_____

_____

_____

_____

4

CHARACTER AND REPUTATION

Substance over Form

A father wanted to inculcate a sense of responsibility in his careless son. So he told his son that for every careless act of his he would hammer a nail into a wooden pillar in their house, and for every positive act he would pull out one nail at the end of the day. The boy saw that the pillar was getting crowded with nails. He resolved to change his behaviour and the nails started coming out, till there were none left. The father was very proud. He said, "Son, you have done a great job, there are no more nails left on the pillar." The boy, however, started crying and replied, "The nails are gone but the holes remain."

There are a few morals to this story:

➢ Some mistakes are a part of the learning process and may be unavoidable.

➢ Mistakes, even when corrected, leave marks forever.

➢ Some mistakes are just not correctable and the price paid is very heavy. For example, carelessness while crossing the street can cost a life.

➢ Ignorance does not spare anyone nor is it an excuse for not meeting adult obligations.

➢ Experience is a good school, but the fees can be pretty high.

*I*t is not to say that one can't ever make a mistake all through life. In fact, if you do know someone who has never committed a mistake, then you know someone who has never done anything anyway. Making a mistake is not the end of the world but repeating, defending and lying about it can spell disaster. Wise people learn from their mistakes, but wiser people learn from other people's mistakes because our lives are not long enough to make all of our mistakes and learn.

Let not life become a comb that nature gives us
after we have lost our hair.

Most of our learning takes place during the formative years. It is relatively cheaper to learn the lessons of life at home than to learn them from the world outside. Because at home we are taught, whereas the outside world puts us to test. Often, when children, out of ignorance or defiance, neglect parental warnings, the price tag is very heavy and has to be paid in one's adult life.

"A pat on the back develops character – if administered young enough, often enough, low enough."

– Anonymous

Let's face it – life is not all smooth sailing. The ability to navigate well is the sign of a well-developed character. The difference between ability and character is that ability will get us to the top but character will keep us there. We meet all kinds of people in life, sometimes unfair, unreasonable and unscrupulous people, who are ready to hurt us. No matter how prepared we are, we may still make mistakes. But being prepared softens the blow and limits the damage.

To keep a nation strong and free,
There are some things that must always be,
So long as values and characters are kept alive,
A nation and the people will always survive.

– Author unknown

Nations and civilisations are built on character.

What is Character?

Character is not a gift, it is an accomplishment. Character is built bit by bit through hard work. It is a combination of many qualities. The key qualities of a person of character are trustworthiness, ethics and high morals.

People of fine character live by their values. They are honest and are committed to truthfulness in thought, word and deed. True character thus encompasses the capacity for self-discipline.

People with character rely on their integral value system to differentiate between the right and the wrong. Character is easier kept than regained. Character creates self-respect, which in turn leads to high self-esteem.

Maturity is reflected in all aspects of character – the decisions we make, the friends we choose and the responsibilities we accept.

Charisma and Character

Character is more important than charisma. How many times have we gone to a store to buy something and found the salesperson likeable but somehow not trustworthy? We come back without making the purchase. There is a difference between personality and character. We may like or dislike personalities but it is their character that we trust. Personality opens the door but character keeps it open.

*Bill Clinton enjoyed one of the highest popularity rat-
ings for a President in the US. And yet, in 2001, the
US Supreme Court debarred him from practising law.
He was seen as less than an ideal candidate for the
Chancellorship of Oxford University for the fear of the
"dubious" message it would send to others.*

[*Source: Asian Age,* 2 October 2001; *Hindustan Times,* 14 Janu-
ary 2003]

The misconduct of people in positions of power is
more harmful than that of those not in power. Why?
Because people look up to them. They are the centre of influence and impressionable people accept
such behaviour as the norm or a justification to do
wrong leading to degradation.

Reputation and Character

Reputation is what other people think of us and
character is what we know who we are. The following incident explains it.

We were expecting to be paid $5000 on an
invoice for services performed, from a
client in California. Finally, after many reminders, we got paid after six months.

Surprisingly on the same invoice a month later, we
received a second cheque.

When my secretary received the second cheque, she
walked into my office and said, "Do you remember
the people who kept us waiting for a payment for six

months? And finally sent the cheque last month. Well, now we have a second cheque from them. What should we do?"

Doesn't she know what is to be done with the cheque? Why did she come to me? She came in to check my pulse!

I asked her, "What would you do if I was not here?" That settled it.

We had a few choices:

➤ We could have deposited the cheque and the client might never have found out and we could have been $5000 richer. But did we earn it?

➤ We could have deposited the cheque and may be after a year or two, in their internal audit the client may have found out that they made a double payment and called us, bringing the mistake to our attention. We could have acted surprised and said, "Oh really! We will check our records and get back to you," even though we knew they were right straightaway. The next day we could call back and say, "Oh yes, we did receive your second cheque. It was a mistake and we will return the excess payment." We appear honest, but are we really?

As far as the other person is concerned, even after a year or two, all it took was a phone call to us and they got the money back. We are building a reputation of honesty. But are we really honest.

➢ The right option was to make sure that we are not making a mistake, because we don't want to chase them again, and if it is, actually an excess payment, send the cheque right back.

The above incident brings out the difference between doing the right thing for the right reason vs doing the right thing for the wrong reason. Some people are honest because they believe that's the right thing to do. Whereas some people are honest because they do not want to get caught telling lies.

Houses that look alike from outside may not be similar within. One may have a weak foundation and get blown away by the slightest wind. The other may have an unshakable foundation, and withstand great adversity. It is the same with character. Just like no lasting structure can be built on a weak foundation, a worthy and fulfilling life cannot be built on a weak character.

Character is about good values, discipline and a sense of responsibility. It has many benefits, the most endearing being that it fosters harmony in every area of one's life.

In order to understand better the distinction between character and reputation, I have drawn the following list:

Reputation	*Character*
Reputation is what other people think of us.	Character is knowing who we are.
Reputation is the picture.	Character is the reality.
Reputation may be a camouflage.	Character is the truth.
Reputation may be damaged by others.	Character can only be damaged by oneself.
Reputation is a bonus.	Character is an achievement.
Reputation invites admiration.	Character invites trust.
Reputation is the exterior.	Character is the interior.
Reputation is the image.	Character is the substance.
Reputation may be manipulated.	Character is constant and reflects the core values.
Reputation may be an overdraft.	Character is your bank balance.
Reputation may reflect strength.	Character is seen in the right use of strength.
Reputation may be gained by one act.	Character is built by many actions.

Reputation may grow like mushrooms.	Character grows like an oak tree.
Reputation may be built by brain and beauty.	Character is built on values and vision.
Reputation is fragile like a glass.	Character is strong like a foundation.
Reputation may be inherited by you.	Character is what your descendents inherit.
Reputation can be made by what others fall for.	Character is built by what you stand for.

Personality and reputation are like images that people see and judge us by. It may be a beautiful, fragile camouflage that attracts people to us, but shatters quite as easily if lacking substance. If reputation is glamour, then character is actuality, based firmly on knowledge, truth and trust. The fact that reputation is temporary can be seen by the rapidity with which it changes. On the other hand, no one but you can destroy or build your own character. Personality or reputation without character will fall apart sooner or later. How long can you carve a rotten wood?

CHARACTER IS SUBSTANCE OVER FORM

We need substance to live honourably. Some people value respectability and status symbols more than relationships. Flashy exteriors cannot for long hide the cheapness of the character inside.

Have you noticed how a piece of furniture made from inferior quality wood does not take polish? No matter how much you polish, the grain does not show. On the contrary, good quality wood reveals its grain with just a little polish. This is true of character – its strength provides the basis for a lasting image.

The quality of an organisation or a country depends on the moral character of its people. Moral character and principles are the basis upon which individual lives are built. Nothing, not even science and technology can do away with the need for character.

CHARACTER – NATURE OR NURTURE?

Character is not something we are born with. It is a learnt behaviour. Our values come to our aid when we face the world.

> *"In each of us, two nations are at war, the good and the evil. All our lives the fight goes on between them, and one of them must conquer the other. But, in our own hands lies the power to choose – what we want most to be, we are."*

> – Jekyll and Hyde Club, established 1931,
> New York City

A complete training of the head and the heart is needed to build a sound character. Life is a moral and spiritual journey. It does not make sense to hope that we will stumble onto something that will eventually generate lasting values. Good and strong character is the result of practising good behaviour with discipline.

When we find ourselves on unfamiliar grounds, it is our character that helps us identify our own and other people's strengths and weaknesses. It gives us the wisdom to identify what's good for us. Again, it is character which teaches us what to look for and what to overlook, when to fight and when to walk away, when to take advice and when to make one's own decisions.

"Character comes from following our highest sense of right, from trusting ideals without being sure they'll work."

– Richard Bach 'One'

Maintaining character is like maintaining an automobile. For smooth running, it needs constant upkeep. Having to work to overcome temptation stops at the point in life when character wins decisively. Character building takes place minute by minute and is revealed at the time of crisis. An athlete keeps practising and reveals his preparedness at the time of competition. In the same way a person does not build character at the time of crisis. Rather, he shows his preparedness.

A person of sound character would not do wrong even if he knew he would not get caught.

THE MAN IN THE GLASS

When you get what you want in your struggle for self,
   And world makes you king for a day;
   Just go to a mirror and look at yourself,
   And see what that man has to say.
   For it isn't your father or mother or wife,
   Whose judgment upon you must pass;
   The fellow whose verdict counts most in your life,
   Is the one staring back from the glass.
      Some people may think you are a
         straight-shooting chum,
      And call you a wonderful guy;
   But the man in the glass says you're only a bum,
   If you can't look him straight in the eye.
   He's the fellow to please, never mind all the rest,
   For he's with you clear up to the end;
   And you have passed your most dangerous,
         difficult test,
   If the man in the glass is your friend.
   You may fool the whole world down your
         pathway of years,
   And get pats on the back as you pass;
   But your final reward will be heartache and tears,
   If you've cheated the man in the glass.

– Anonymous

ACTION PLAN

Rules to live by for building an honourable character:

1. Become labelled as trustworthy – a person of integrity.

2. Don't cheat.

3. Don't steal – Never take anything without asking. Borrowing without permission is stealing.

4. Choose your friends carefully – You reveal your character not only by the company you keep, but by the company you avoid.

5. Don't try to buy friendship – Try to stay away from people who do that. Friendship is not for sale.

6. Associate with people of the highest character.

7. Choose your direction based on values – Do the right thing for the right reasons. Practise goodness because that is the right thing to do.

8. Live by the philosophy – always give more than expected – go the extra mile. Always give more than you get paid for.

9. Keep your commitments. Don't let people down.

10. Seek responsibility, not control.

11. Find happiness by helping others – Go out of your way to do something for somebody.

12. Learn to maintain confidentiality – Do not disclose anything told in confidence.

13. Don't speak ill of people behind their backs – It shows poor character.

14. Constantly strive to keep your conscience alive.

15. Don't pre-judge people – Get all the facts. We accept or reject people based on their lifestyles. Lifestyles can be deceptive.

16. Be yourself. Don't pretend. Avoid being a phony – but this does not mean you show your worst side. Don't take pride in your negatives. Strive to improve but don't put yourself down.

17. Help others. You won't succeed because others fail – Have a helpful attitude. To help, one has to go out of their way. It doesn't happen by the way. Helpfulness is not an exchange of favours. It is incidental to friendship and must be practised.

18. If you make a mistake, say you are sorry. Be patient when someone makes a mistake. Don't re-experience other people's mistakes. Learn from them and avoid your own. Mistakes are certain, misery is optional.

19. Make your parents proud –

They are counting on you. Be thankful to your parents for all they have done. It is a great heritage to have honest parents. Leave a legacy for your children.

20. Always use soft words and hard arguments and not the reverse.

21. Sincere 'please' and 'thank you' never go out of style – stay away from meaningless and phony pleasantries.

22. Practise good listening. Don't interrupt and don't complete other people's sentences.

23. Be gentle. It is a sign of strength – Only the weak are cruel.

24. Self-worth is more important than net worth.

25. Beware of rumours and gossipmongers – Keep your conversation on a positive tone without malice or envy. Abstain from loose and frivolous talk. Don't laugh or take pleasure in other people's misfortunes. Don't make fun of

others even when the occasion arises.

26. Stay occupied – Build a community that benefits everyone at large. Find a cause or a hobby. It is relaxing.

27. Read a good book every week. It enriches your soul.

SELF-EVALUATION
SHEET

_____

_____

_____

_____

_____

_____

_____

_____

_____

_____

_____

_____

_____

_____

_____

_____

_____

_____

5

LEADERS OR MISLEADERS

Good Leaders Guide,
Bad Leaders Misguide

*T*here is an ancient Indian story about the mother
who asked her Guide, "Is life tough?" The
Guide said, "Yes, it is. But, if you do the right
thing the end is better than the beginning." The mother
looked at her children and thought to herself, "Nothing
could be better than seeing these kids grow up to be
good adults with the right values."

Night came and the children were afraid. The mother
pulled them closer. The children said, "Mother, so long

you are here with us, we are not afraid of anything." The mother thought, "Nothing could be better than seeing my kids grow up to be courageous."

The next day, all of them were climbing up a hill. The mother encouraged her children, saying, "With a little more effort and patience, we will be up there." They all reached the top and the children said, "Mother, we could not have done this without you." That night, the mother looked at the stars and said, "Nothing could be better than this day, because my children have learned determination with which to face obstacles in life."

The next day there was a storm. The mother told her children, "Look beyond the clouds and see the bright sunshine." The children looked up and saw beyond the darkness. That night the mother got down on her knees and prayed, "Nothing could be better than this day because I have given my children the ability to see beyond darkness."

Years went by, the mother became old and weary as her children became tall and strong. Their character and courage shone through as they supported their mother when the path was tough and she needed help.

At last, the day came when the mother had to leave the world. She said, "I have reached the end of my journey and now I realise that the end is better than the beginning, because my children can walk alone and then their children after them."

The children said, "You will always walk with us mother, even when you are gone." As they saw their mother leave the world, they said to one another, "A mother like ours, even in passing away, is not a memory, but a presence. She may be invisible but she is always by our side."

That's leadership – it's leaving a legacy – a legacy that prepares others to carry on with courage, determination, and the ability to see the larger picture.

True leadership is the ability to be a catalyst for change, to inspire and persuade people to follow the righteous path. A leader puts ideas into people's minds and inspires them into action. Empowering one's followers rather than controlling them is the hallmark of true leadership.

A father's sacrifice empowers a daughter to face the world.

A DAUGHTER'S LOVE

Her hair was up in a ponytail
Her favourite dress tied with a bow.
Today was Daddy's day at school,
And she couldn't wait to go.

But her mommy tried to tell her,
That she probably should stay home.
Why the kids might not understand,
If she went to school alone.

But she was not afraid;
She knew just what to say.

What to tell her classmates
Of why he wasn't there today.

The little girl went to school,
Eager to tell them all.
About a dad she never sees
A dad who never calls.

One by one the teacher called,
A student from the class.
To introduce their daddy,
As seconds slowly passed.

At last the teacher called her name,
Every child turned to stare.
Each of them was searching,
For a man who wasn't there.

"Where's her daddy at?"
She heard a boy call out.
"She probably doesn't have one,"
Another student dared to shout.

And from somewhere near the back,
She heard a daddy say,
"Looks like another deadbeat dad,
Too busy to waste his day."

With her hands behind her back,
Slowly she began to speak.
And out from the mouth of a child,
Came words incredibly unique.

"My daddy couldn't be here,
Because he lives so far away.

But I know he wishes he could be,
Since this is such a special day.

We used to share fudge sundaes,
And ice cream in a cone.
And though you cannot see him,
I'm not standing here alone.

"Cause my daddy's always with me,
Even though we are apart.
I know because he told me,
He'll forever be in my heart."

With that, her little hand reached up,
And lay across her chest.
Feeling her own heartbeat,
Beneath her own favourite dress.

And from somewhere in the crowd of dads,
Her mother stood in tears.
Proudly watching her daughter,
Who was wise beyond her years.

And when she dropped her hand back down,
Staring straight into the crowd.
She finished with a voice so soft,
But its message clear and loud.

"I love my daddy very much,
He's my shining star.
And if he could, he'd be here,
But heaven's just too far.

You see he was a fireman
And died just this past year.

When airplanes hit the towers
And made the meaning of freedom very clear.

But sometimes when I close my eyes,
It's like he never went away."
And then she closed her eyes,
And saw him there that day.

And to her mother's amazement,
She witnessed with surprise.
A room full of daddies and children,
All starting to close their eyes.

"I know you're with me daddy,"
To the silence she called out.
And what happened next made believers,
Of those once filled with doubt.

Not one in the room could explain it,
For each one of their eyes had been closed.
But there on the desk beside her,
Was a fragrant long-stemmed pink rose.

And a child was blessed if only for a moment,
By the love of her shining bright star.
And given the gift of believing,
That heaven is never too far.

– Anonymous

A father left a leader even after he was gone.

A true leader works at creating more leaders, not followers. A leader inculcates in people the desire to carry on the mission after he is gone. It takes internal security and competence to create new leaders. Leadership is another name for moving confidently on a firm foundation.

WHAT IS LEADERSHIP

Leadership is not about making emotional speeches and leading demonstrations. Leadership involves trust. And only those inspire trust who have the ability to subordinate their ego to the greater good. Mahatma Gandhi, had no guns or money, but he had the power to move hundreds of millions of people. He had their trust and they walked behind him.

Leadership is often demonstrated when the chips are down and the odds are against us. If Columbus had turned back, he would not have been blamed, but then he would not have been remembered either. All great leaders have displayed great perseverance. A leader's personal example acts as a catalyst in inspiring others to follow him.

One of the strongest desires that a follower has is to be identified with his leader. The leader who gives that identification to his followers acts as a motivating factor for them. There is no such thing as a neutral leader. Leaders are either good or bad, effective or ineffective. Good leaders guide and lead, bad leaders misguide and mislead.

People are looking to emulate leaders who are living and breathing examples, not idealised characters from a work of fiction. Leaders are to their followers what hope is to the hopeless.

ONLY A DAD*

Only a dad with a tired face,
Coming home from the daily race,
Bringing little of gold or fame
To show how well he has played the game:
But glad in his heart that his own rejoice
To see him come and to hear his voice.

Only a dad but he gives his all,
To smooth the way for his children small,
Doing with courage, stern and grim
The deeds that his father did for him.
This is the line that for him I pen:
Only a dad, but the best of men.

– Edgar Guest

Leadership is not only demonstrated in the battle-field or in times of crisis but in everyday deeds. For example:

➢ A mother raising four kids on a small income.

➢ Parents teaching good values to their children.

➢ A person initiating to get the neighbourhood garbage dump cleaned.

➢ A person leading a campaign to build ramps for physically challenged children in schools.

---

* From *The Book of Virtues for Young People*, p. 320.

> A person helping the elderly or invalid to cross the street.

> An individual offering to carry a heavy bag for an old lady.

These are the unsung leaders of everyday life. It is only when you become willing to assume a greater share of your responsibility towards yourself, your family, organisation and the community that you assume the status of an everyday leader.

The challenges of daily living can be daunting. But leadership is not about quitting. It is about creating the right environment and building the right spirit. Leadership is about respecting the spirit of action and standing for a cause.

WHEN WAS THE LAST TIME *YOU* TOOK A STAND?

Leaders take bold stands. Cowards on the other hand avoid situations that challenge them. Our life is not determined by where we are but by what we are. We go along with people to get along because we are looking for comfort and not accepting challenges. We seek approval more than respect.

Standing in the middle of the road is very dangerous; you get knocked down by the traffic from both sides.

– Margaret Thatcher

Why are People Afraid to Take a Stand?

Because it is inconvenient. So long as people prefer convenience to conviction society always goes downhill. People who are afraid to take a stand prefer to play it safe all the time. They are wishy-washy and hence not trustworthy.

> *If a man hasn't discovered something he will die for, he isn't fit to live.*
>
> – Martin Luther King

Some people don't want to accept responsibility or the accountability that goes with it. They find it easier to make excuses and blame the world. It's just never their fault. They prefer security rather than struggle. They feel "I am too weak and helpless and the problem too strong. I cannot make a difference." They become comfortable with misery. They put up with misery simply because they are afraid of change.

Take a Stand

No useful contribution to society has ever been made without taking a stand. There is a fine line between firmness and stubbornness; fame and popularity.

Taking a stand means that you take and maintain a firm position for or against an issue.

All through history when great leaders have taken a stand they have been willing to accept and suffer pain. They have been tortured, burnt alive, exiled and shot, but they have not compromised on the larger interests of society. They believed in the philosophy that it's not the number of years you live, but the principles you stand for in your life that is important. Good leaders do what's right rather than what makes them look good or popular.

The search for cheap popularity at the expense of morality, ethics and honesty amounts to looking for honours without honour. What is popular is not necessarily right and what's right need not always be popular.

Stand with anybody that stands right; stand with him while he is right and part with him when he goes wrong.

– Abraham Lincoln

Churchill demonstrated great leadership and courage during the Second World War.

"We shall go on to the end. We shall fight in France, we shall fight on the seas and oceans, we shall fight with growing confidence and growing strength in the air, we shall defend our Island, whatever the cost may be. We shall fight on the beaches, we shall fight on the landing grounds, we shall fight in the fields and in the streets, we shall fight in the hills; we shall never surrender."

– Winston Churchill,
Address to the House of Commons, 4 June 1940

CREDIBILITY GAP

Why is there a credibility gap and distrust in today's leaders? It is because their promises amount to nothing more than lies. Some leaders change their principles for position; others change their positions for their principles.

The devil can cite scriptures for his purpose.

– William Shakespeare

Followers can and do easily recognise a phony leader, often called a pseudo leader. Now, you might ask, if people recognise a phony leader, why do they support him? How do dishonest politicians get elected? There are a number of reasons.

Most often, it is a choice between two evils. People prefer a known devil to an unknown one. They are looking for the lesser of two evils – which in reality may not always be the case. When they knowingly elect the wrong person, it is not because of trust but because they are going in for a trade off. What they don't often realise is that they are only trading an imaginary gain for long-term pain.

Cowards can never be moral.

– Mohandas Karamchand Gandhi

In an environment of uncertainty, people usually look for short-term gain. They feel short-term gains prepares them to handle long-term uncertainty.

People who elect dishonest leaders to public offices for personal gain don't trust such leaders themselves. They need to ask themselves two questions:

➤ Would they appoint these people as guardians of their children?

➤ Would they appoint these people as trustees of their estate?

If the answer is 'NO' then anyone who supports a dishonest leader is behaving irresponsibly, being anti-social, and is as much an accomplice to the crimes of that leader as the criminal himself.

Someone asked a priest, "When you see a politician do you pray for him?" The priest replied, "No, when I see a politician I pray for the country."

WHAT IS GOOD LEADERSHIP?

The concept of good leadership has not changed over time. Given below are elements of distinction between Pseudo Leaders and Great Leaders that guide their behaviour:

Pseudo Leaders	Great Leaders
position	action
control	support
authority	mentoring

technical expertise	people expertise
talk	listen
tell	ask
self-centred	relating well to others
gives order	gets input
scare	inspire and motivate
secretive	inform and enlighten
wait for consensus	create consensus
assume communication	get feedback
scheme	plan
manage things	lead people
keep power	empower
intimidate	coach
drive	lead
rely on reputation	rely on character
look for short-term gain even at the expense of long-term pain.	accept short-term pain for long-term gain.

Citizens may not mind sacrificing for a cause or the country but they certainly wouldn't want to sacrifice anything for a dirty politician.

HOW DO WE RECOGNISE A PSEUDO LEADER?

A surgeon, an engineer and a politician died and

went up to the gates of heaven. St. Peter was waiting for them. He said, "There's been a mix up somewhere; our accounting department didn't realise we were supposed to get only one person. Now we have got three and we cannot really accommodate that many. How do we figure out who is allowed in?" After much debate it was finally decided that the person belonging to the oldest profession would be the one to enter heaven.

Right away the surgeon jumped up and said, "It's got to be me. Creating Eve from Adam's rib was a feat of surgery. It had to be done by a surgeon. Therefore, I belong to the oldest profession." "Wait a minute", the engineer said. "It couldn't be you. Before God created Adam and Eve, there was chaos. And creating order out of chaos is a work of planning that can be accomplished only by an engineer. Therefore, it's got to be me before you." At this the politician jumped up and said, "Both of you stay behind. WHO DO YOU THINK CREATED CHAOS?"

Pseudo leaders are generally without conscience. Their greed prompts them to indulge in misdeeds, causing irreparable damage to society. Pseudo leaders are more like partners in crime. They trust each other only out of convenience and self-interest and prey on each other during times of crises.

Pseudo leaders take a stand till opposition appears and then they change or run. A pseudo leader is like a wolf in sheep's clothing. He's wrong but he looks right.

Pseudo leaders perceive value as something disposable if the price is right.

Once George Bernard Shaw asked a socialite if she would spend a night with him for a thousand pounds. The socialite snapped and said, "I am a respectable married woman. How dare you have the guts to ask me that!" Bernard asked, "How about ten thousand pounds?" This time she exploded threatening to call her husband. Still persistent, he offered a million pounds with the assurance that nobody would ever find out. This time, she said 'perhaps'.

"What if I were to offer you only ten pounds?", he asked. "Mr Shaw, you are insulting me!", the woman was shocked. "Who do you think am I?"

"We have already established who you are," he pointed out calmly, "Now we are only haggling over the price."

Pseudo leaders cannot resist the highest bidder. He believes in honesty – when he is bought, he stays bought. The more he claims that he is honest, the more firmly one should hold onto one's wallet. He gives publicly and steals privately. He has a magnetic personality in that he pulls one's money like a magnet. They believe in public works programmes in which *they* get the money and the public works. It is not unusual for pseudo leaders to behave like dogs for the sake of a bone. A pseudo leader is the kind of person who would murder both his parents and then plead for mercy on grounds of being an orphan. The lack of ethics in pseudo leaders is the root cause of the destruction of living with honour.

To a pseudo leader power is potent and money is omnipotent.

He has a million-dollar smile – he smiles only at millionaires. When you lend him money, he tells you truthfully: "I shall remain indebted to you forever." When he borrows money, it's not only against his principle to pay interest, it is also against his interest to pay the principle. If you want to learn the difference between capital and labour, lend him money: The money you lent him is the capital, while struggle in getting it back is labour.

He stands for everything that he thinks others will fall for.

The main emotions that motivate most politicians are:

Fear	Jealousy	Hate
Anger	Greed	Revenge
Superstition	Insecurity	Indecision
Doubt	Ego	

A pseudo leader has a mind of his own!

Pseudo leaders have minds like concrete – all mixed up and fixed forever. The narrower the pseudo leader's mind, the broader his statements. A pseudo leader runs a large-scale operation with a small-scale mind.

He cannot be called a cheap politician.

Pseudo leaders will stoop to any level for cheap popularity even when that involves compromising on their morality, ethics and integrity. Pseudo leaders would tilt the country to balance the budget.

When he asks you to support him and a good government, he is asking you to vote twice: once for him and the second time round for a good government. His time is divided between running for office and running for cover.

How are Politicians Different from Statesmen?

- Statesmen look for breakthroughs while politicians thrive on breakdowns.

- Statesmen generate cooperation, confidence and creativity. Politicians generate confusion, conflicts and controversies.

- Statesmen strategise, politicians dramatise.

- Statesmen lead, politicians mislead.

- Statesmen improve the lives of others; politicians improve their own bank balance.

- Statesmen direct and strengthen their character, politicians misdirect and corrupt their followers.

- Statesmen dream, politicians scheme.

No wonder the game dirty politicians play is called Politics. If you bifurcate the word into two you will get:

- poly means many, and
- tic(k)s are blood sucking bugs

So, 'Politics' = Many blood suckers.

The management philosophy of a politician is:

Source of energy	:	greed
Vision	:	whats in it for me
Management style	:	looking for trouble and finding it everywhere
Sense of justice	:	protecting the guilty, punishing the innocent
Sense of motivation	:	rewarding the incompetent
Source of strength	:	chaos and confusion

Stubborn Like a Donkey.

A farmer once had two donkeys. He wanted to find out which of them was more stubborn than the other. So he tied the two with a 15 ft rope. He put two stacks of hay 25 ft apart and let the donkeys loose. Each donkey started pulling towards its own stack of hay. After tugging, pulling, tugging, pulling, they started choking each other. But they were donkeys. They continued pulling in their own direction and eventually choked each other to death. They could have both gone together in one direction and eaten one stack of hay and then gone to the other and eaten that too. But they didn't do it that way. Why? Because they were donkeys. They choked each other to death.

The sad part is, there are many donkeys who exist in human form. When some of them get into positions of power they cause irreparable damage to society.

Pseudo leaders are a part of our everyday life. You may come across them personally or professionally. They may even be too close for comfort – a friend or a relative perhaps?

They believe in law and order, so long as they can lay down the laws and give the orders.

They are always looking to advance politically by bribing, appeasing, seducing, confusing, manipulating and threatening people. When a pseudo leader asks for advice, he is actually looking for an accomplice.

They think of securing their seat rather than securing their country. Their solutions are usually worse than the problems. Followers fake loyalty to pseudo leaders and then pull the rug from under their feet.

A civilisation is not destroyed by barbarian invasion from without, but it is destroyed by barbarian multiplication within.

– Will Durant

True leaders not only love the truth for its own

sake but also despise deceit. They understand that falsehood can be far more painful than the hardships that accompany honesty.

"Lives of great men all remind us
We can make our lives sublime,
And, departing, leave behind us,
Footprints on the sands of time."

– Henry Wadsworth Longfellow

ACTION PLAN

Ask yourself the following questions:

1. Can people trust me?
2. Am I doing the best?
3. Am I committed to the task?
4. Do I care about the others?

If the answer is 'Yes' to all the above, you have the ingredients of a good leader.

Here is the outline of an action plan for good leadership:

- Get Involved – Life is not a spectator sport. You have no right to criticise the system unless you get involved.

- Volunteer to Accept Responsibility – Take initiative rather than wait for someone to give you responsibility.

- Serve – If you want to be a great leader, learn the joy of serving. Identify three areas where you could serve others.

- Be Prepared to Take a Stand – Identify three areas where you would take a stand. That means taking a risk for what you believe. It takes moral courage.

- Evaluate Yourself – Ask yourself how do you rate against the criteria mentioned in this chapter.

SELF-EVALUATION SHEET

_____

_____

_____

_____

_____

_____

_____

_____

_____

_____

_____

_____

_____

_____

_____

_____

_____

SELF-EVALUATION
SHEET

6

LEADERS ARE FOREVER

Leave a Legacy

*L*eaders who leave a legacy are those who start out on their journey with great ideas and a a deep sense of commitment. Genuine leaders think not only of today but tomorrow and the day after. Such leaders change the course of history.

The history of the world is full of men who rose to leadership by sheer force of self-confidence, bravery, and tenacity.

– Mahatma Gandhi

Just as Cream Rises Above the Milk, Leaders Emerge.

It is not uncommon to see people stopping by the scene of a car accident simply to 'have a look'. All of a sudden, one person comes along and takes charge of the situation. He gets one person to call an ambulance, another the police, checks out the injuries, and gets the ball rolling. Who gave this person authority? No one. But you will notice that the way he conducts himself, he gets people to start obeying him. He empowered himself by accepting responsibility and taking charge. ***Leadership is about taking initiative and being accountable.***

By definition, leadership means having the power, whether institutionalised or informal, to lead. The question is, where does a leader get power from?

Sources of Power for Leaders

1. *Power by Position:* Positions and titles give power. Take away the title and the power goes away. ***Position gives authority and authority gives power but only good behaviour begets respect.*** The people most obsessed with titles and status are usually the least deserving. Any

title, position or power, unless it is built on justice, cannot endure. Political pseudo leaders, especially, are spineless and can walk only with the help of the crutch of authority. Greatness does not lie in just being strong but equally in the right use of that strength.

2. *Power by Proxy:* This is power that is given or received through a process of delegation by a higher authority. Getting power through authority does not guarantee that it will be used appropriately and not abused.

3. *Power by Personality:* This is often referred to as charisma. But the razzle-dazzle of a charismatic personality can blind us only for a while. When we wake up, if our hero lacks substance, he doesn't look any good anymore.

4. *Power by Proficiency:* Also known as exceptional ability, proficiency in any particular field can give limited power and possibly respect depending on behaviour.

5. *Power by Principle:* This flows from our value systems, beliefs, courage, conviction and integrity.

The winning combination of leadership is personality and principles put together. In other words, charisma and character. The same principles apply in our personal life. We get married to personality but we have to live with the character.

Power Corrupts and Absolute Power Corrupts Absolutely.

Many people believe this statement to be true but there's another side to it. Some of the greatest leaders in the world did the greatest good from positions of power. They chose not to succumb to the temptation to abuse their authority and become corrupt even when they were clearly in positions where they had both the temptation and the opportunity. How is it that they didn't become corrupt? George Washington was offered bribes to betray his country. He refused. Why don't good leaders become corrupt? The answer is that they are not corruptible. Power does not necessarily corrupt. Power only corrupts those who are corruptible to begin with. However, when the corrupt get into positions of power, they corrupt power itself. For them politics is the art of acquiring and holding on to power.

Many people say that with success comes arrogance. The converse is equally true. There are many people who, the more successful they are, the more humble they become. Does success bring arrogance or humility? It does neither. It unmasks the person and only brings to the surface whatever was hiding before.

Contrary to the above, sometimes a successful person's firmness can be misconstrued as arrogance and their politeness and humility perceived as weakness.

Being powerful is like being a lady: if you have to tell people you are, you are not.

– Margaret Thatcher

Authority is Not Enough

Authority is not a substitute for leadership. Leaders who can inspire others always outperform pseudo leaders who depend on authority. The power in authority is fear motivation. The best it can do is generate compliance, not good will. People will not stretch wholeheartedly beyond compliance. Authority blinds a pseudo leader and he does not realise that it is to be saved for an emergency. A good leader is looking for cooperation not just compliance. A true leader inspires and earns respect. Pseudo leaders let power go to their head. They display authority unnecessarily and lose respect. Pseudo leaders treat the symptoms not the system.

A society is in danger when those who have never learnt to obey are given the right to command.

Pride and Humility

There is nothing noble in feeling superior to some other person. The true nobility is in being superior to your previous self.

– Indian proverb

One quality of a good leader is that while his pride is reflected in his work, he himself practises humility. What does that mean? Taking pride in your work entails setting high standards for yourself and not being satisfied till you surpass those standards. This pride comes from an awareness of your capabilities and from a burning desire to increase or extend them.

The true leader instils this same pride in his team. How does he do that? When things go right, a good leader is humble enough to give credit to the team. And when things go wrong, he accepts responsibility.

PRIDE and HUMILITY are both satisfying and gratifying whereas VANITY brings bitterness, discontentment and disgruntlement.

VANITY

When people feel that they deserve more than what they have got and they actually don't – that's vanity.

Vanity is false pride. False pride makes people ridiculous. Insincere praise to somebody with low self-esteem brings a swollen head that is vanity. Vanity shuts the doors on help and leaves the curtains open to the display of stupidity.

HUMILITY

When people feel that they have got more than what they deserve and they actually do – that's humility.

When you pretend to be humble, you have lost – humility only comes naturally. Sincere deserving appreciation needs to be accepted and acknowledged with sincere gratitude. That's humility. When a person feels he is unworthy of sincere appreciation, it would be either that meritoriously he feels undeserving or his low self-worth does not permit him to accept the appreciation.

PRIDE

When a person feels that they got what they deserve because that's what they earned – that's pride.

The champion, when he wins the gold, wears it with great pride. He doesn't say I don't deserve it. Athletes spend 15 years training for 15 seconds of performance. They never say I don't deserve it. But they have the humility to give credit to those behind the scene. Could he have ever won the gold without a good coach, mentor or the support of his family? Never. He does not have the vanity to take the credit. However, the best coach and the support of the family would not get the medal without the effort of the athletes. ***Pride leads to self-confidence whereas conceit leads to arrogance.*** There is a fine line dividing confidence and conceit and the moment you cross it, you lose strength.

Humility is Respect for Humanity

In India, there is a traditional greeting called "Namaste". It is done by folding both hands together, bowing your head slightly and saying "Namaste". It means, "The divinity in me salutes the divinity in you." It is a sign of humility.

Self-respect does not mean that I deserve more respect than others. Basic courtesy and manners are also a part of respect and dignity besides learning and training.

Many years ago at Chicago Railway Station, senior officials and reporters were awaiting the arrival of a Nobel Prize winner. As the big man got off the train, cameras were flashing furiously. City officials were stretching to shake hands and tell him how honoured they were to meet him. Having thanked them, he excused himself for a moment, walked briskly through the crowd and picked up the bags of an elderly woman who was struggling. He escorted her, carrying her bags to the bus and wished her a safe journey. He then came back to the crowd and said, "Sorry to have kept you waiting." The man was the world famous Dr Albert Schweitzer. Having seen this, a member of the reception committee said to one of the reporters, "That's the first time I ever saw a sermon walking."*

---

*Adapted from *More Sower's Seeds: Second Planting*, Brian Cavanaugh, T.O.R. Paulist Press, Mahwah, p. 47.

True humility is invisible and helps build others. Humility either comes naturally or it looks contrived. The tree bends when it bears fruit. Humility is a sign of maturity. Take successes in stride, have a big heart instead of a swollen head.

Humility, however, does not mean self-demeaning behaviour. That would amount to belittling oneself or considering oneself unworthy. Humility is nothing else but plain, simple, decent, down-to-earth behaviour.

Why is Humility Important?

People who let success go to their heads are resented. Leaders should look for cooperation and goodwill rather than the acknowledgement of their superiority. A good leader doesn't feel the need to flaunt his authority. He is not trying to impress anyone. He doesn't suffer from insecurities or complexes. Good leaders are not arrogant. Flaunting authority and displaying arrogance distances the leader from his team and his followers.

Leaders who take pride in their work are the most humble about their achievements. *Humility does not mean that people think less of themselves; it only means that they think of themselves less.*

Difference between Leadership and Management

Both management and leadership can be learned.

Good leadership cannot be learnt without trials. A manager may or may not be a good leader. Some of the world's greatest leaders such as Churchill, Alexander the Great, and Henry Ford did not go through any formal leadership or management programmes. Honourable living requires leadership qualities regardless of our position or profession in life.

> *The manager administers, the leader innovates.*
> *The manager maintains, the leader develops.*
> *The manager relies on systems, the leader relies on people.*
> *The manager counts on controls, the leader counts on trust.*
> *The manager does things right, the leader does the right thing.*
>
> – Fortune Magazine

I don't think the demarcation is as clear as defined above. One can have and needs elements of both.

A good leader commands the highest respect because he is trustworthy, dependable and gives strength and courage to those around him. The success of a leader is determined not by how much wealth he accumulates but how many hearts he continues to live in after he is gone.

Leadership is a Combination Not a Key.

A safe cannot open with a single number; you must

have the right combination of numbers to be able to open it. Similarly, one quality is not enough to make a leader. A leader must have the right balance and combination of vision, values, competence, courage and character. One without the other will not work. A good leader is both a coach and a cheerleader.

Very often, a good worker gets promoted to become a supervisor. The functions of a supervisor and a worker are quite different. A person who is a good worker may not necessarily be a good supervisor and if that happens, then the company has lost on two accounts:

➤ They have lost a good worker, and

➤ They now have a bad supervisor.

Leadership principles seem simple once they are revealed, just like a magician bedazzles his audience with his tricks, but once he tells them how they are done, it all seems really obvious.

Successful people are not just go-getters but go-givers. They give their best, and because they give their best, they get the best from others. They realise life is a boomerang. The more they give, the more comes back.

Leaders aren't born leaders. Leadership qualities can be acquired.

LEADERSHIP: ESSENTIAL IN EVERY SPHERE OF LIFE

A headless institution does not work. Every family, community, country needs a leader.

As responsible adults, we are called upon to assume leadership roles in our day-to-day lives. Directly or indirectly, actively or passively, we all influence someone, somewhere, in some manner, shape or form – for the better or worse. Followers have the responsibility to expect high standards from their leaders. Strong commitment to principled action and service is the responsibility of every person. The willingness to address fundamental issues and then make every effort to live by the answers is what makes a great leader great.

If we are not part of the solution, then we are the problem.

Corrupt exploiters, with insatiable greed, are forever looking for new opportunities to destroy society for their personal gain. **When worthy people do not come forward to take on positions of leadership, an ugly breed of self-serving parasites fills the void.**

People with leadership skills sometimes refuse public service and leadership roles because they are content with their status and wealth. In this way, they don't enforce a status quo but bring degradation.

They put their conscience into deep sleep. Their indifference encourages cynicism in those around them. This laid-back attitude, however, serves as an opportunity for arrogant and selfish pseudo leaders to fill the vacuum.

Honourable Living and Politics

People come to me and say, "I keep to myself. I want to have nothing to do with politics. I don't want to be involved." How absurd? We are already involved, by not being involved. The air we breathe, the water we drink, the food we eat, the education our kids get, the taxes we pay, the medicine we take, our very existence is the result of politics. How then can we not be involved? We are already involved – either by choice or by default. Life is not a spectator sport. And when we fail to get involved we also lose the right to criticise.

A Leadership Creed

I believe in the supreme worth of the individual and in his right to life, liberty, and the pursuit of happiness. I believe that every right implies a responsibility; every opportunity, an obligation; every possession, a duty. I believe that the law was made for man and not man for the law; that government is the servant of the people and not their master. I believe in the dignity of labour, whether with head or hand; that the world owes no man a living, but that it owes every man an opportunity to make a living. I believe that thrift is essential to well-ordered living and the economy is a prime requisite of a sound financial structure, whether in government, business, or personal affairs. I believe that truth and justice are fundamental to an enduring social order. I believe in the sacredness of a promise, that a man's word should be as good as his bond; that character, not wealth or power or position, is of supreme worth. I believe that the rendering of useful service is a common duty of mankind and that only in the purifying fire of sacrifice is the dross of selfishness consumed and the greatness of the human soul set free... that right can and will triumph over might.

– John D. Rockefeller Jr

Remember

A person who cannot lead and will not follow invariably is a troublemaker.

Either lead, follow or get out of the way.

– Ted Turner

SELF-EVALUATION
SHEET

ACTION PLAN

1. Identify your present source of power.

   _____

   _____

2. Identify three behaviour patterns that you would like to adopt in order to assume a leadership role.

   _____

   _____

   _____

3. Identify your motivation to be a leader. Is it to satisfy ego or some society? That is what distinguishes between a leader and a misleader.

   _____

   _____

   _____

SELF-EVALUATION SHEET

_____

_____

_____

_____

_____

_____

_____

_____

_____

_____

_____

_____

_____

_____

_____

_____

_____

_____

_____

7

CORRUPTION

Parasites in the System

> France fell because there was corruption without indignation.
>
> – Romain Rolland

ccording to an ancient saying, the longer one waits to fight evil, the harder it is to defeat it.

Once, in spite of repeated warnings from his neighbours, a man planted a thorny bush in the middle of a path. As the bush grew larger it started hurting the passersby. Every time someone asked the man to remove the bush he postponed it for another day. Then, one day he was himself wounded by a thorn and started bleeding. Now, he wanted to get rid of the bush but he was helpless. It had become too large for him to pull it out.

As the above story indicates, *evil, if not destroyed at the outset, keeps growing stronger even as you become weaker in comparison.*

The story of the thorny bush is like a parable for the growth of corruption in a society. Like the thorny bush, someone somewhere is responsible for planting the seed of corruption. As citizens, most of us, like the man in the story, ignore the little sapling of corruption until it becomes a big thorny bush that endangers our well-being, one that we are helpless against.

Unless we destroy the seed of evil, it will destroy us.

WHAT IS CORRUPTION?

Corruption is the evil desire to exploit the unfortunate, the defenceless and the vulnerable. The heartless intensity of corruption is often the result of devious planning. *In a corrupt society, laws are like spider webs that catch the weak and the poor but can be destroyed by the rich and the powerful.*

Corruption unchecked is like cancer that will eventually eat out the social order from within.

Often the sheer scale and magnitude of the problem encourages superficial minds to be satisfied with the notion that corruption has and will always be with us. People justify its presence as a global phenomenon. No society has ever attained 24 carat purity in honesty and integrity. But how can we ignore the difference between 22 carat and 8 carat purity? Is corruption, then, the exception or the rule?

In corrupt governments, positions are created for men, whereas in good governments, men are chosen for positions that exist.

Once a minister (politician) from a corrupt third world country went abroad on a personal invitation from a minister from another nation. He was surprised at the extravagant red carpet welcome. After a while, he asked his host how he managed to extend such an expensive reception without any state sponsorship. The man took him to the window and pointing out to river, said "Do you see that river?" and the answer was "Yes." "Do you see that bridge on the river?" and the answer was again "Yes." The minister said, "10 per cent."

Then, the next year, the minister from third world country invited his counterpart to his own country and threw an even grander welcome. The man, though flattered, was surprised and asked him how he could manage such opulence without support from the state. The minister smiled and took his perplexed friend to the window and asked: "Can you see that river?" and the answer he got was "Yes." Then he asked, "Do you see the bridge on the river?" and the answer was "No." The minister said: "100 per cent."

In corrupt societies when a person sees inhuman treatment, he sometimes wonders if this world was created by God or the Devil (when God was not looking).

Corrupt democracy means that gangsters run the country in uniform and terrorise the honest citizens. A corrupt government is nothing less than organised crime. Whenever a corrupt government official says, *"I am from the government and I am here to help,"* you know you have a problem on your hands. Officials are supposed to be the servants of the public but their way of functioning suggests that the public has become the servant of the corrupt.

The preservation of a government depends on the faithful discharge of duties by its citizens. If citizens neglect their duties and place unprincipled men in office, the government will inevitably become corrupt.

In a corrupt system, laws are made for self-interest not public interest, and most importantly, corrupt and incompetent men will get appointed to positions of power. Public revenues are squandered, the rights of citizens violated and ignored. When the government itself breaks the law, it breeds general contempt for law in society.

With degradation of values, ill-gotten wealth become the criteria of status and respect. We are not talking here of piecemeal corruption but of entire system that becomes corrupt and affects all areas of a citizen's lives. When corruption becomes a way of life, freedom loses its meaning. A society succumbs when corruption attains epidemic proportions. Honourable living is threatened.

It is important to recognise that corruption thrives because of a sleepy conscience.

There was a man who thought that if he stole a little wheat from different farms, the other farmers would not notice it while he would have a big pile of wheat for himself. One night he went to the farms and asked his daughter to stand guard while he went stealing. As he was stealing from the first farm, his daughter shouted, "Dad! Someone is watching you." He came running out, but saw no one there. He then went to the second farm to steal some more wheat. Again, his daughter called, "Dad! Someone is watching you." He came out running but again he saw no one there. Then he went to the third farm. For the third time, his daughter cried, "Dad! Someone is watching you." As before, he came running back but saw no one again. This time he got angry. "Why do you keep shouting that someone is watching me, when there is no one here?" His daughter replied, "Dad, there is someone who is always watching you from above and that is GOD."

God is often another name for one's conscience. It is one's only guardian in moments of moral crises. It is the inner voice, which guides us in the right direction. To the corrupt and the dishonest, a sleepy conscience is a source of great happiness and comfort. People who betray others actually betray their conscience first. When a person betrays his conscience, his conscience may be silent but it is never secure.

The greatest moral degradation lies in exploitation, which takes place under the guise of virtue. *Societies like these resemble rotten fruit, which surely have worms inside.*

George Bernard Shaw said, "Democracy substitutes election by the incompetent many for appointment by the corrupt few."

The word "commissioner" acquires a special meaning in a corrupt society. It's evident that a fire commissioner takes commission on every safety certificate that he grants, a housing commissioner takes commission on every house that is built. The income tax commissioner takes a commission on every income. Commissioners in corrupt societies live on commissions. No wonder in such societies, anyone who takes commission is called a commissioner!

Gradual Degeneration

What happened to the label?

The degeneration of a society is not surprising when corruption becomes acceptable and no stigma is attached to a corrupt person. Social stigmatisation of the corrupt in the past served a useful purpose; it quarantined such people from the rest of the society to ensure its moral good health. People didn't want to socialise with the corrupt nor did they want their children married into families that were corrupt, as the label was looked down upon. But today, with the general degradation of values, we justify our acceptance of corrupt practices by saying, "You have to be practical." Corruption is not an end but a means to an end, the end being wealth, power and authority. *A corrupt country runs like a bus where half the passengers are trying to drive the bus and the other half are trying to collect the fare.*

The link between crime and corruption is deep-seated. Extortion, bribery, rape, treachery, murder, plunder, selling of public offices, embezzlement become a part of daily life. Corruption is the biggest obstacle in fighting crime. Corruption can be compared to terrorism: its victims don't bear names. Acts of corruption are unaddressed letters directed to "whom it may concern".

WHAT IS THE SOURCE OF CORRUPTION?

Sources of corruption are easily seen by all:

- Bad laws
- Bad men

Nothing destroys respect for the government more than having laws in place which cannot be enforced. Bad men, much more than bad laws are responsible for corrupt practices because, after all, it is they who create bad laws. In a society, there are people of:

- High moral values
- Low moral values

Experience shows that a small percentage of people, no matter how bad the laws are, practice ethical behaviour. The reverse is also true – a similar percentage would cheat no matter how good the laws are. However, the majority rely on the system to give them direction. In a good system, a corrupt person has a hard time; whereas, in a corrupt system, an honest person has a hard time.

Corruption, though can never be eliminated, can be minimised. The corrupt, regardless of where they are, find devious ways to corrupt the system.

There was once a king who had a crooked minister, a man who would make corrupt gains regardless of his postings. When the king became aware of his activities, he thought of an infallible solution and posted the minister by the ocean to count the waves, thinking that corruption would cease. He didn't however realise the ingenuity of the crooked minister. The minister started collecting money from the boatmen and the swimmers on the pretext that they were obstructing and interfering with his official duties by disturbing the waves.

When people who lack moral values obtain positions of power they endanger society. That is when corruption becomes rampant.

CAUSES OF CORRUPTION – NEED OR GREED

Scarcity – Corruption can result from scarcity of essential goods where demand is high and supply is low. This imbalanced function of demand and supply may be real or artificially created for ulterior gains.

Abject Poverty – For the sake of survival, a person has to resort to corrupt practices.

Acquire wealth – To meet the objectives of luxurious living, people resort to corruption. Wealth attained by foul means helps people achieve high positions in a corrupt society and they are actually looked up to. When crime starts to pay, as it does in a corrupt society, it is given a more respectable name.

The corrupt are a part of the human race with a human face, lacking in humanity.

FORMS OF CORRUPTION

Gifts – an official accepting gifts given with the objective of influencing him to give undue advantage to the giver.

Extortion – the demanding of gifts or money by an official is extortion. The official is saying – "Unless you pay me, I'll make your life hell!"

Embezzlement – siphoning of funds.

Nepotism – where appointments of relatives are made regardless of their merit. To a corrupt person, Einstein's "Theory of Relativity" is getting their relatives on the payroll!

Regardless of its form, corruption involves:

- Subordination of public interest to private gain
- Breach of trust
- Secrecy; lack of transparency
- Violation of duty and public welfare
- Deception
- Disregard of national welfare

CONSEQUENCES OF CORRUPTION

- Corruption devastates smooth administration.
- Corruption is the cause of brain drain.
- The morale of the nation and its citizens is adversely affected.

- Corruption has a snowballing effect.
- When corruption grows, so does crime.
- Corruption does not let its citizens either live or die with dignity.
- Corruption leads to lack of humanity and compassion.

HOW DO WE FIGHT CORRUPTION?

Concerned citizens must come into decision-making positions and

- pledge their commitment to eliminate corruption and injustice.
- create strong and honest leadership who will guide the citizens and the nation through this process.
- check the lure of easy money and power through a strong judiciary.
- must feel the absolute need to work towards enhancing their moral character and destroying the evil influences of corruption from the root.
- Form and support honest pressure groups to bring transparency and accountability into the system.
- Create a national movement against corruption by educating citizens of their social obligations.
- Be prepared to sacrifice in the struggle for

humanity as opposition will come from vested interests.

Every time we look at our kids, we need to ask will they be its next victims?

The fight against corruption is a struggle for survival between the corrupt and the patriotic. Strong public opinion needs to be created against this social disease. Good citizens have to come out of their apathy and become intolerant of corruption.

As most individuals become part of the corrupt system, corruption becomes a culture and that culture is best described as vulture-culture. It is a dog-eat-dog situation. When people have been abused at some point in their lives, then they too learn to abuse when they get into positions of power. The culture in any society goes top down and never bottom up. A small act of corruption usually triggers off a chain reaction. It creates an economic problem and that creates further corruption. Slowly, corruption becomes not only a part of the industry but an industry by itself. *Real problems arise when corruption seeps into the working of the government and the hearts of the people.* A nation's vulnerability coupled with its citizens' complacence brings the situation to a point of no return. Corruption begets still more corruption and the cycle goes on endlessly. It generates a whole new breed of people called touts, contact man, go-betweens who thrive on victimising and extortion. Sycophancy and yesmanship then become an integral part of culture.

A Jelly fish sometimes swallows a snail. The snail because of its shell stays protected and alive inside the jelly fish. To sustain itself, the snail starts eating the jelly fish from inside and keeps growing. A day comes when it consumes the entire jelly fish and the jelly fish is no more.

Corruption does the same thing to a nation. It eats from within till the nation is **NO MORE**.

History stands witness to the fact that those who cut their country's throat end up cutting their own.

ACTION PLAN

1. Resolve to fight against corruption.

2. Identify three areas of your life where corruption is hurting the system.

   _____

   _____

   _____

3. Start generating public opinion through a social group to clean the system.

SELF-EVALUATION
SHEET

_____

_____

_____

_____

_____

_____

_____

_____

_____

_____

_____

_____

_____

_____

_____

_____

_____

_____

_____

_____

8

TEACHING HONOUR

Influence Eternity

Our youth does not form 100 per cent of the population but they definitely form 100 per cent of the future of society.

The youth of a country are the leaders of tomorrow. The future judges, the generals, the politicians and the doctors – are sitting in the school and colleges of today. The future of the nation depends on their knowledge, their character, skills and their preparedness or lack of it.

A honourable nation emerges when citizens build their character. It is said that the first lessons in character-building begin at kindergarten. To me, it starts even earlier – not when a child is born, but a hundred years before. Why? Because attitude and values are genetic – they go from one generation to the next.

There was an elderly person planting some acorns. A man passing by asked, "Old man, look at your age. Do you think you will live long enough to see the oak trees." And the man replied, "All the trees that have given me shade and fruits – did I plant all of them? There are people coming behind me too."

Aren't we custodians of the next generation?

A nation behaves responsibly when it treats the assets of the nation in trust for the next generation.

Habits contracted at a young age are generally permanent, and influence conduct throughout the life. If during the formative years time is misspent, the chances are that it has been lost forever. There is no compensation for the time lost in one's youth.

The debate in any community cursed with crime

today is not the punishment of criminals but the prevention of the young from being trained in crime.

In many societies, the young person of today faces an identity crisis. Evident through self-doubt and despair. His despondency reflects the moral and ethical void at the heart of society. We need to realise that young minds are more impressionable than mature minds.

We cannot prepare the future for our youth but we can certainly prepare our youth for the future.

This is where caring parents, teachers and custodians of society need to get involved. It is without doubt important for children to get good academic training but the values parents teach their children are more important for real success.

The greatest gift my parents gave to me. . . were their unconditional love and a set of values. Values that they lived with and didn't just lecture about. Values that included an understanding of the simple difference between right and wrong, a belief in God, the importance of hard work and education, self-respect and a belief in America.

— Colin Powell

Accountability and Direction
Generally, it is assumed that parents have unconditional love for their children. I wonder what

unconditional love means? Does it apply to all relationships or only parent-child? Or are there no exceptions? Does it mean a spouse should accept infidelity or get beaten up unconditionally? Does unconditional love mean that we let one family member who is a drug addict sacrifice the interest of the entire family? The way I see it: if one partner becomes sick or disabled, the other spouse has not only made a commitment to look after that person, but also that he or she would not look for physical and emotional gratification outside marriage because that would be dishonourable. The word commitment and unconditional have a common meaning which says, "I'll stand by you, no matter what." It doesn't say, "I'll stand by you only in good times or till I find a better one." Unconditional love implies sacrifice. At the same time, it makes allowances for imperfections, as none of us is perfect. We need to accept each other with the good and bad. If a loved one goes off track, our responsibility is to bring him on track. However, in spite of the best efforts, if he doesn't come on track for whatever reasons and if the issue is value-based, one needs to re-evaluate the relationship.

It is not uncommon to see parents sacrifice their needs in order to meet their children's wants. However, being accepting does not relieve a parent of their responsibility to make their children accountable for their behaviour. Just because children do not always heed the right advice does not absolve parents of their responsibilities. *Parents who are afraid to put their foot down usually have children who step on their toes.* Some parents bring their children up while others let them down.

The best security blanket that parents can provide to a child is in the form of role models who respect each other. *A breakdown of the values in the family amounts to a breakdown in the life of the youth.*

The young generation is the first thing that comes to our minds when we think of a breakdown of values. We say, "look at the younger generation and their values." We use the term "delinquent teen-agers" for them. The question we need to ask is "who is delinquent – are they or are we? And, more importantly, who is to be blamed?" The following poem clarifies as to who is delinquent.

Ready and eager to act, the youth today have become synonymous with impatience. They need guidance, for if left directionless, their youth becomes a blunder, their manhood a struggle and their old age one of regret. Since lessons of good values transcend generations, when you inculcate good values in your children, you are really teaching good values to your grandchildren also.

WHO IS TO BLAME?

We read it in the papers and hear it on the air
Of killing and stealing and crime everywhere.
We sigh and we say as we notice the trend,
This young generation . . . where will it end?

> *But can we be sure that it's their fault alone?*
> *Are we less guilty, who place in their way*
> *Too many things that lead them astray?*
> *Too much money, too much idle time*
> *Too many movies of passion and crime.*
> *Too many books not fit to be read*
> *Too much evil in what they hear said.*
> *Too many children encouraged to roam*
> *Too many parents who won't stay home.*
> *Kids don't make the movies, they don't write the books*
> *They don't paint the pictures of gangsters and crooks.*
> *They don't make the liquor, they don't run the bars,*
> *They don't change the laws, and they don't*
> *make the cars.*
> *They don't make the drugs that muddle the brain;*
> *That's all done by older folks . . . eager for gain.*
> *Delinquent teenager; oh how we condemn*
> *The sins of the nation and blame it on them.*
> *Instead of placing blame, let's fix the cause,*
> *And remember as we pause;*
> *That in so many cases – it's sad but it's true –*
> *The title "Delinquent" fits older folks too!*

> – Anonymous

The wife of one American President and the mother of another, Abigail Adams was a prodigious letter writer in her day. In the following letter written to her son John Quincy in the winter of 1779-80, she makes her conviction uncompromisingly clear.

My Dear John:

Improve your understanding for acquiring useful knowledge

and virtue, such as will render you an ornament in society, an Honour to your Country and a Blessing to your parents. Great learning and superior abilities, should you ever possess them, will be of little value and small Estimation, unless Virtue, Honour, Truth and integrity are added to them. Adhere to those religious sentiments and principles which are early instilled into your mind and remember that you are accountable to your Maker for all your words and actions. Let me enjoin it upon you to attend constantly and steadfastly to the precepts and instructions of your father as you value the happiness of your Mother and your own welfare... I had much rather you should have found your Grave in the ocean you have cross[e]d or any untimely death crop you in your Infant years, rather than see you an immoral profligate or a Graceless child.

[Source: *Great Letters in American History* by Rebecca Price Janney, Pennsylvania: Horizon Books, 2000, Page 54]

Discipline doesn't break a child's spirit but lack of it breaks a parent's heart.

It is a parent's duty towards society to make his child valuable member of that society.

Paul Harris, whose vision of Rotary shines today over 150 countries and inspires the hearts of over a million Rotarians globally, credits his grandparents for instilling in him the values that eventually became the foundation of Rotary. This only shows that the ripple effect of good parenting is limitless. Their influence affects eternity.

Boundaries or Bondage

A parent ought to be able to distinguish between boundaries and bondage. Call them rules or limits, good ones are essential to serve a purpose and are an expression of a loving concern. It is a parental duty to see that children experience the true consequences of their conduct. Growing up honourably is difficult for a child whose parents don't give him enough importance. Parents, who do not expect proper behaviour from their child and don't discipline him, actually do not respect him enough to teach him honourable living. In our current so-called free or liberal culture and permissive atmosphere, the idea that a person ought to be accountable for his behaviour may seem old fashioned. If a young child sticks out his tongue or uses profanity, and a parent casually or approvingly ignores the insult, or addresses it lightly – can they claim to have a fine child? Their unspoken protection amounts to an encouraging of aggression.

Children obey parents, but wherever parental values are weak, the parents obey their children. A problem child reveals problem parents. Indisciplined children when young may disturb your sleep but when grown up they can disturb your life. Discipline is an act of love.

Education – Character or Academics

There are two kinds of education – one that helps you make a living and one that makes your life.

The real end of any education is to build character and help develop good citizens of tomorrow.

To know how to read is not as important as to know what to read.

Education is the progressive discovery of ones ignorance. Learning how to learn is the basis of education. It directs our choice between right and wrong. It is a good system of education which inculcates the principles of humanity.

Education is the soul of society. It teaches us to respond to tradition by neither rejecting it nor accepting it slavishly. Education teaches us the rules and exceptions and thus influences the thinking of the future generations.

Nature brings out the distinction between man and brute, and education brings out the difference between one man and another.

In order to make the people protect their rights and responsibilities, mass education needs to be prioritised. *It is education which makes people easy to lead but hard to drive, easy to govern but hard to enslave.* To them freedom takes priority over privilege or security. They understand that a society can never be free till all the principles of freedom have been adopted.

Character building always remains the prime purpose of education. This helps people live prosperous just, and dignified lives. This process though has two steps:

1. Self-education and self-development – which is an individual development.

2. Societal development – collective development of all individuals in a society.

Our children have the right to expect from society:

➢ Fairness, justice and equal opportunity to utilise one's abilities as each citizen chooses.

➢ A system of education that gives each citizen a sense of social responsibility.

These goals are achievable. All it takes is commitment to education.

Countries are not built by bricks but by minds. If you find education expensive you ought to try ignorance! You will see for yourself, which is more expensive.

What is the essence of an educated person? William Arthur Ward of Texas Wesleyan University identifies the following ten hallmarks of an educated person:

THE TEN HALLMARKS OF AN EDUCATED PERSON

1. Educated persons think clearly and logically, live honourably and courageously, give willingly and generously, and forgive lovingly and graciously.

2. They are keenly aware that responsibilities have higher priorities than privileges; that freedom is more precious than security.

3. They realise that their learning is never complete; that life is a never-ending process of growth.

4. They understand that simplicity is the essence of beauty, and that personal integrity is the cornerstone of character.

5. They understand that great ideas are more permanent than great wealth; that excellent examples teach more than polished phrases.

6. They recognise that curiosity is the wick in the candle of learning, and that wonder is the flame that lights the torch of adventure and achievement.

7. They have developed inner reservoirs of thankfulness and learned creative ways of expressing their gratitude to their Creator and their fellow humans.

8. They welcome, respect and enjoy new challenges, different cultures, unusual customs and opposing opinions.

9. Educated persons are those who thirst for additional knowledge, hunger for more truth, and yearn for increased wisdom.

10. They recognise their limitations but focus on the possibilities. They appreciate their uniqueness but celebrate their oneness with all humanity.

– William Arthur Ward

The reason why many parents and teachers no longer inspire the younger generation is that they are themselves going the wrong way – embracing a culture of self-gratification by declaring "It's my life".

A teacher affects eternity.

In ancient India, a student would live with his teacher as a member of his family. The teacher took on the entire responsibility of shaping his student in lieu of fees. To the student, the teacher's status was akin to that of God. Learning cannot take place without respect for the teacher. A teacher can be a mother, a schoolmaster, or a principal. Anyone who imparts education is a teacher. If genius is the gold in the mine, then a great teacher is like the miner who works to bring it out.

Teachers are the makers of history.

Honour in Marriage – A Preparation for Life

Marriage is usually referred to as holy matrimony, acknowledging that the relationship is sacred. Marriage is not just a contract between two people, it is a sacred covenant.

Today's society is constantly redefining morality and dragging it gradually towards permissiveness, self-centredness and clubbing everything under the umbrella of being non-judgemental in society.

"The Bible distinguishes between holy and unholy sex. Holy sex is that which takes place between the husband and wife in fulfillment of their marital relationship. Unholy sex is everything else. Sexuality and obligation are intimately connected. Adultery comes from the term *adulterate* which means to contaminate or to make impure. Adultery is also a form of theft. Adultery affects the stability of the family, undermining the trust of husband and wife and threatening the integrity of the family unit.

According to a 1994 University of Michigan study, 'infidelity is indeed the primary cause of divorce.' Dr. Frank Pittman, an internationally renowned expert on sexuality and marriage states that in his thirty-seven years of experience as a therapist, he has encountered only two cases of first marriages ending in divorce in which adultery was not involved.

According to Dr. Lana Staneli, author of a book on marital triangles, 'Of those who break up their marriage to marry someone else, eighty percent are sorry later. Having an affair is an invitation to an awful lot of pain and tragedy'."

[Adapted from the *Ten Commandments* by Dr. Laura Schlessinger; Harper Collins Publishers, Inc., 10 East 53ʳᵈ Street, New York, NY 10022.]

Some of the greatest leaders in the world not only inherited their values from their parents but felt a very strong obligation to impart them to the next generation.

Former President of USA, Mr Ronald Reagan to his son at the time of the latter's marriage.

Dear Mike:

You've heard all the jokes that have been rousted around by all the "unhappy marrieds" and cynics. Now, in case no one has suggested it, there is another viewpoint. You have entered into the most meaningful relationship there is in all human life. It can be whatever you decide to make it.

Some men feel their masculinity can only be proven if they play out in their own life all the locker-room stories, smugly confident that what a wife doesn't know won't hurt her. The truth is, somehow, way down inside, without her ever finding lipstick on the collar or catching a man in the flimsy excuse of where he was till three a.m., a wife does know, and with that knowing, some of the magic of this relationship disappears. There are more men griping about marriage who kicked the whole thing away themselves than there can ever be wives deserving of blame.

There is an old law of physics that you can only get out of a thing as much as you put in it. The man who puts into the marriage only half of what he owns will get that out. Sure, there will be moments when you will see someone or think back on an earlier time and you will be challenged to see if you can still make the grade, but let me tell you how really great is the challenge of proving your masculinity and charm with one woman for the rest of your life. Any man can find a twerp here and there who will go along with cheating, and it doesn't take all that much manhood. It does take quite a man to remain attractive and to be loved by a woman who has heard him snore, seen him unshaven, tended him while he was sick, and washed his dirty underwear. Do that and keep her still feeling a warm glow and you will know some very beautiful music.

If you truly love a girl, you shouldn't ever want her to feel, when she sees you greet a secretary or a girl you both know, that humiliation of wondering if she was someone who caused you to be late coming home, nor should you want any other woman to be able to meet your wife and know she was smiling behind her eyes as she looked at her, the woman you love, remembering this was the woman you rejected even momentarily for her favours.

Mike, you know better than many what an unhappy home is and what it can do to others. Now you have a chance to make it come out the way it should. There is no greater happiness for a man than approaching a door at the end of a day knowing someone on the other side of that door is waiting for the sound of his footsteps.

– Dad

P.S.: You'll never get in trouble if you say "I love you" at least once a day.

Acceptance of values results from exposure to what is acceptable in society. One night stands and purely physical relationships degrade the sanctity of love and the relationship. Animals do not have sacred relationships. They engage in instinctive procreation. The feeling of satisfaction or shame comes from the sanctity of the relationship.

When we use adultery as a slapstick tool for laughter in TV shows showing feelings of hurt and betrayal are of little consequence. What message are we giving to the viewers? Think about it.

Assets or Liabilities

How do we teach wrong values in our organisations and our families?

A phone call comes to my office. If I cannot take the call, my staff will not lie and say I am not there.

If a creditor calls our office saying that he hasn't received a cheque that was due to him, our staff would not lie that the cheque is in the mail if for some reason we did not send the cheque. If I teach my secretary to lie for me, a day would come when she would lie to me too. One day she wants to go shopping and calls in sick. Perchance, I also happen to go out shopping the same day, see her and ask, "I thought you were not well." Pat comes the reply, "Yes, I wasn't but I just took two aspirins. I am feeling much better now!" Who taught her to lie? I did. Now she has become an expert liar. I did a pretty good job, didn't I? This is how we teach wrong values in our organisations. Does the above sound familiar?

Now, lets take the case of family. I am sure you will agree that children are not born liars. They learn. A child answers the phone enthusiastically. The caller asks, "Can I talk to your dad?" The child replies, "Of course." He goes running to his father and says "Dad, there is a call for you." "Who is it?" The child gives the name. The father says, "I don't want to talk to him. Go tell him I am not here." "But, daddy, you are here." "Yes," quips the father, "but go tell him I am not here." "But daddy, you are." This time the father says in a harsh tone – "Do you want me to teach you a lesson? Go tell him I am not here." So, the child goes back, scratching his head and wondering, "Dad is here but he says, 'Go tell him I am not here.' But he is still here." His enthusiasm level comes down because he has never lied before. He is uncomfortable because for the first time in his life he is confused. He does not know what to do. He just wants to get out of the situation. So, he picks up the receiver and says, "Dad says dad is not at home" and bangs down the phone. The father heard that one and gives a knock on his son's head and says, "You just made a liar out of Daddy." Guess, who made a liar out of who? After the child learns his lesson, he says, "No more confusion, Dad. I am clear now. Watch me." Next time the phone rings and somebody asks for his father, he says, "I'll check." He goes running to his Dad and says, "Dad, call for you." "Who is it?" asks dad: so-and-so. Before dad can say a word, the child says, "Dad, you don't have to talk to him. I'll tell him you're not here'. Daddy says, "Son, I want to talk to him." The child says, "No dad, you don't have to." Look at what happened. Even before daddy says a word, the kid is ready to lie for daddy. Does this happen in many homes or am I exaggerating? Right from childhood, the child is learning to tell little, little lies and by the time, he grows up, he has become what – an expert liar! He has perfected the art of telling lies.

It may be extended to stealing, cheating, whatever. Practice does not make perfect. Practice only makes permanent whatever you practice. Only perfect practice makes perfect. Some people keep practicing their mistakes and they become perfect in making mistakes. Every time the kid does something wrong like lying, stealing, cheating, he falls down a little in his own eyes, his self-esteem goes down and his inferiority complex goes up. It is worth repeating, this is universally true that whenever a person does something wrong like lying, stealing, cheating, even if no one is watching, his self-esteem goes down. The converse is true too. And whenever we do something positive, even if no one is watching, we rise a little bit in our own eyes. That is the magic of self-esteem.

Many times people justify lying by saying 'this is only a small lie. When the big one comes, I'll tell the truth'. In reality, when we practice telling enough small lies, when the big one comes, we end up telling a bigger lie. Why? Because that's what has become permanent. Similarly, when we practice cowardice enough times consoling ourselves that when the big ones comes, I will show courage. But when the big one come, what happens? We end up showing cowardice. Because thats what we practiced and it became permanent. Remember practice does not make perfect. Practice only makes permanent whatever we practise. Only perfect practice makes perfect.

Another Real Life Situation

A man has two children aged six and ten. He goes to the State park and sees at the ticket counter a sign saying, "Children under five go free." Right before reaching the ticket counter, he tells his younger one, "If the ticket clerk asks your age, tell him it is quarter to five." We teach our children to lie for two bucks.

The example below shows how a parent teaches good values.

There is another man with two kids aged six and ten. He sees the sign too but proceeds to ask for one adult and two tickets for children. The cashier looks at the younger one and asks how old he is. The father says, 'six'. The cashier is amazed and says, "if you hadn't told me, I would have never have known. He could have easily passed for under-five". The father replies, "You would have never come to know but my son would have." Guess whose kids are more likely to become good adults?

I repeat, we teach our kids to lie for two bucks. Once they grow up, they would sell their conscience for two bucks.

Many parents are too busy to be parents at all. Hence, they compensate by being friends to their children and forgetting their responsibility as a teacher. They blame schools not realising that schools generally reinforce values taught at home. Many television programmes show examples of kids being smarter than their parents and show parents as stupid. While growing up, we were taught to respect and behave, appropriately. Respecting parents is a childs responsibility and behaving worthy of respect is the parental obligation.

The younger generation believes in a new social philosophy, i.e. "respect must be earned' and that 'respect is no longer presumed but granted." However, we were brought up with a different philosophy that our parents, teachers and elders are worthy of respect till they prove unworthy. Some cultures, however, practise that a person is not deserving of respect unless they have earned it.

Respect is not the only element in holding a parent in high regard, but translates into behaviour towards them, that reflects their status as parents, in spite of your opinion about them. Acts of caring demonstrate honour as does refraining from actions that would embarrass them. By not giving them respect, we deny their worth in society.

This is the story of a grandfather who lived with his children and grandchildren. They enjoyed having their meals together. As years went by, grandfather's health declined and his hands became unstable. Sometimes he spilt the food which became rather messy. One day, in the presence of some guests grandfather dropped the dish. His son couldn't take it any more. Rather annoyed he said, "I can't put up with you any more. In future you have to sit by yourself and eat alone in your room." He gave his father a wooden bowl that would not break. The elderly man now labelled as the "old man" was barred from coming to the dining table. Loneliness was his only companion. One evening when the son came home, he saw one of his sons busily carving a wooden bowl. He asked his son, "Who are you making this bowl for?" The son replied, "Dad! This bowl is for you." Shocked, the father asked why of all things he needed a wooden bowl. To this, the son replied, "I'm preparing for the future. When you become an old man and start spilling your food, you won't be allowed to eat with us any more. You will then need this wooden bowl to eat your meals alone in your room." The father quietly walked away with feelings of realisation and remorse. He went straight to his father's room and said, "Dad, I am sorry for what I have done to you. You took care of me all my life no matter how clumsy I was. You never made me eat my meals alone. I apologise for not giving the due respect and dignity that you deserve. Please forgive me."

That night the "old man" became an elderly father and sat at the table like before enjoying dinner with his family. Though the table got messy, nobody minded it any more. Any culture that honours its elders is civilised in its true sense.

A parent-child relationship is unique and irreplacable. Strangers do not place the same demands as parents do. Its not uncommon to see a 50-year old feeling like a child in the presence of his parents.

Honouring parents is one way to ensure that the elderly are suitably rewarded and feel wanted in society. It is a single thread that connects the two generations. And, if ever, a need comes to correct the parent, the objective is to do without putting them down.

Children of weak and immoral parents can bring honour to their parents by their actions of doing good to the world.

"Yes" and "No" Generation

In order to teach children the right values, parents need to learn to say "NO" to kids.

We are the "No" generation. "No" Generation represent people above the age of 50. What does that mean? It means that whenever we asked our parents for anything, they said, "NO". By looking at their eyes, one could tell that when they said "No", they meant "No" and "I better not ask again". Today's generation are the "Yes" generation. Anytime they go to Mom or Dad and say, 'Can I buy this?' The answer is "Of course". 'Can I do this'? "Yes"! Can I go to a restaurant? "Of course"! And if per chance, in his life he gets a no, the child looks straight into his parents eyes and says, "why", and regardless of the answer there is another why and the next and then the next. By the seventh why, most parents give up and say "Okay". Is this kind of interaction familiar? When you see an interaction like this, what's the first question that comes to mind – "Who is the parent?" The next question is – does a four year old have the same maturity as a forty year old? Sometimes, we can answer all the Whys and the child still may not understand, so the appropriate answer is "because, I say so". Why are we afraid of saying, "because we say so". Even though our parents kept saying "no" and we keep saying "yes" to our kids, we realise we respected our parents much more than our kids respect us.

People who have never learnt to obey can never learn to command.

Many times, we keep buying expensive things for our loved ones thinking we are giving them gifts, they may not be gifts at all, they may only be apologies for the gifts that we never gave them.

To my mom:

You taught me to do what's right when I took a candy without permission at the age of three. You taught me that humanity is more important than an individual. You taught me that integrity was more important than grades. You taught me that acts of kindness are natural outcome of love. You taught me that values are more important than fortunes. You taught me that the tougher decisions are between what's right and more right. You taught me that faith can move mountains. You taught me the importance of giving help to the less fortunate. You taught me to stand by my commitments by staying committed. You taught me that reading was more important than watching television. You taught me that laughing was better than crying. You taught me that honour was more important than honours.

You taught me by example. I love you, mom.

At my seminars, I have heard parents say to me, its so long as my kids are happy doing whatever they are doing that all that matters. I ask them "Don't you want to know what makes your kid happy?" If beating up people on the street and taking their things away gives them happiness, then their behaviour is described by a word in the English language called "perversion". Happiness is important, no doubt, but the source of happiness is equally, if not, more important and the source depends on our value system. Many times, parents keep saying "everything within limits is okay." The question is – is stealing within limits okay? Is cheating within limits okay? Is lying within limits okay? Is adultery within limits okay? Are drugs within limits okay? There are some things in life that are *just not* okay.

I LOVED YOU ENOUGH

I loved you enough to make you save your own money to buy a bike even though I could afford to buy you one.

I loved you enough to let you discover that your new best friend was a creep

I loved you enough to take a Milky Way (even with a bite in it) back to the drugstore and tell him that you stole it yesterday and you were there to pay for it that day.

I loved you enough to stand over you for two hours to have your room cleaned, an act that would have taken me 15 minutes.

I loved you enough to let you see anger, disappointment and tears in my eyes. Children must learn parents are not perfect either.

I loved you enough to let you accept responsibility for your actions, even though the penalties were harsh enough to break my heart.

But most of all I loved you enough to say no when I knew you would hate me for it but those were the most difficult battles of all.

I am glad I won them because in the end you won them too.

– Anonymous

ACTION PLAN

1. Resolve to become a good role model.

2. Identify five behaviour patterns being practiced by you that could be detrimental to members in the organisation and family.

   _____

   _____

   _____

   _____

   _____

3. Do something that would show a caring and respecting gesture to your role models.

4. Identify five behaviour patterns that would embarass your parents if they found out.

_____

_____

_____

_____

5. Practice for a minimum twenty-one days.

9

FREEDOM IS NOT FREE

It is Worth the Price

Before his imprisonment, King Christian X of Denmark, saw the Nazi flag flying on a Danish building. The King called the German commandant and demanded the flag be removed immediately. The commandant refused. The King said, "A soldier will go and take it down." The commandant said, "He will be shot." The King replied, "I don't think so, because I will be that soldier." The flag was removed.

– Christian X (1870–1947)
– King of Denmark (1912–1947)

*T*he honour of the flag represents the ideals it stands for. Upholding this honour is the pride of every citizen.

Balance Sheet of Society

Thinking patterns of individuals collectively form a culture.

A village once initiated a milk collection drive for poor children. It was agreed that before day break every family in the village would contribute a glass of fresh milk. One villager thought, "Since the whole village is contributing, if I put in water instead of milk, it will do no harm, nobody will find out, they would have collected enough milk from others anyway and I will have more for my family." In the darkness of the early morning they all poured their contributions into a common container. At the appointed time when the container was opened in the presence of all villagers, it was filled to the brim. But guess with what – water!

Are you like the villager in the above story? Would you like to live in a village where you have such neighbours? Irresponsible people are more interested in undeserved profits than individual responsibility.

As members of society we are all interconnected. Deceptions by any segment, whether in business or government, may not outwardly appear injurious to anyone but they pollute the system and lower general moral standards.

This raises the question – "Who forms the majority in any country?" Is it the wise or the ignorant? It seems the ignorant generally outnumber the wise. If you go by sheer numbers, then the ignorant shall always rule the wise. What a paradox!

One day a farmer, walking down the street in a small town came across a large stone in the middle of his path. The farmer complained: "Who could be so careless as to leave such a big stone on the road? Why does someone not remove it?" He went away complaining. The next day, the same thing happened with a milkman. He too went away grumbling but left the stone as it was. Then one day, a student came across the stone. Worried that someone may fall over it and hurt himself, he decided to push it aside. He pushed long and hard all by himself and eventually managed to remove the stone from the path. He came back and noticed a piece of paper where the stone was kept. He picked the paper and opened it. Inside was written, **"You are the true wealth of this nation."**

There are two kinds of people – talkers and doers. Talkers merely talk, while doers do. The moral of this story is that if you don't want to get involved you have no right to criticise.

Service to society is the rent we pay for the space we occupy on this earth.

Citizens who forget honour, duty and patriotism invite misery upon themselves and choose to call it divine punishment. We see rampant despair around us but do nothing except pray to God for help. Why would God help those who refuse to help themselves? Self-questioning and introspection are essential to the health of any society. Inaction and irresolution are not empowering for anyone. Sitting helplessly, hoping and waiting for things to happen brings nothing but destruction.

The wealth of a nation is not in material things but rests on the integrity, courage and conviction of its citizens. Service to fellow beings may sound too idealistic, but it is the only way to prove that you care and that goodness exists. *All great nations write their autobiographies through the action or inaction of the citizens. We need to decide whether we are a part of the solution or a part of the problem.* And if we are not a part of the solution, then we are automatically a part of the problem.

> *Nation has passed away and left no traces, and history gives the naked cause of it, one single simple reason in all cases – they fall because their people not fit.*
>
> – Rudyard Kipling (1865–1936)

Detached or Indifferent

Curtailment of desire is seen as a step to content-ment leading to a state of bliss. People have gone to the jungles and the mountains to attain this mental state.

Prime example of detachment in modern times is Mother Teresa who stood up for the poorest of the poor. Her actions were prompted by courage of conviction. She acted with integrity to achieve her objectives. She confronted those who opposed her good work with no regard for recognition or position. She disregarded corrupt authority for the welfare of those who could not fend for themselves. She left her own country and worked in the streets of Kolkata to alleviate the miseries of the forgotten and downtrodden of society. The sheer courage displayed turned this diminutive woman into a giant in the eyes of the world. The world became a better place to live in because of her dedication to humanity.

Hands that serve humanity are a lot better than lips that talk of divinity.

Socrates has said, "I believe that to have no wants is divine." Again, this is detachment not indifference. People who are indifferent in life are people who have failed to live. Often, we see indifference conveniently labelled as detachment.

If INJUSTICE is happening to your neighbour and you can SLEEP, WAIT for your turn because You are NEXT.

Public activity is a citizen's highest responsibility.

Indifference to public welfare is a major cause for collective downfall.

Indifference a Curse

A heart that does not feel pain upon seeing misery and injustice in society is spiritually dead. Watching citizens postpone facing reality is like watching a nation busily gathering material for its own funeral.

The indifference of citizens towards society is the worst curse a society can face.

Indifference is Inhuman

Honourable leaders in the world could have remained indifferent to the injustice around them and called themselves detached. But something bothered them and angered them enough to get them involved. Often, you hear that anger is a sign of weakness. But if you go back in history, you will find that *no change ever took place till somebody got angry.*

Is it not inhuman to see someone's pain and remain indifferent and call it detachment? Is it not one's honourable duty to give voice to the voiceless? A culture of silence in the face of injustice is worse than indifference. *To empathise is to be bothered enough to take action to alleviate another's pain.*

*In Germany they came first for the communists, and
I didn't speak up because I wasn't a communist.
Then they came for the Jews and I didn't speak up
because I wasn't a Jew. Then they came for the trade
unionists, and I didn't speak up because I wasn't a
trade unionist. Then they came for the Catholics
and I didn't speak up because I was a Protestant.
Then they came for me and by that time no one was
left to speak up.*

– Martin Neimoeller

Degenerating Society

In every society some people do not want to work.
Some are afraid of facing up to danger and some
have no love for their community. Such people get
an upper hand in a society that lacks good leadership.

There is a price that one has to pay to stand up
and there is a price that one has to pay for living
on one's knees. Good citizens do not rely as much
on society, as society relies on them.

*For evil to flourish, good people have to do nothing
and evil shall flourish.*

– Edmund Burke

Citizens' loyalty to a country is a payoff in itself.

*In a free country like our own. . . every male brought
into existence should be taught from infancy that
the military service of the Republic carries with it*

honour and distinction, and his very life should be permeated with the ideal that even death itself may become a boon when a man dies that a nation may live and fulfil its destiny.

– General MacArthur

Strength in Unity

There was a flock of quails that lived together in peace. They had resolved that whenever a quail-catcher threw his net to catch them, they would all put their heads out through the mesh and with one force lift off and fly away. Then somehow they would pull themselves out of the net and fly free. The catcher was never able to capture the quails because they were always helping each other. His only wish was that they would start quarrelling. One day, his wish was granted. While landing, one of the quails accidentally hurt another on the head. This made the quail who was hurt angry. The first one apologised but the quarrelsome one continued. "I lift all the weight of the net and you just take a free ride," he charged. This made the first quail angry as well. The catcher saw his chance. Seeing them quarrelling, he threw his net. Too busy arguing amongst themselves, the quails forgot to put their full strength behind lifting the net and the catcher was finally successful in capturing them.

Moral of the Story: An outsider can only take advantage when there was problem within. Till then, he is helpless.

Similarly, in most societies the problems are within.

Well-directed individual efforts can accomplish a great deal. In fact, such efforts encourage other individuals to join in, generating a momentum, which is crucial to bring about change. The dedicated and combined efforts of several people has unlimited potential to improve society. A great river is the sum total of many little streams and rivulets which come downhill, channelling together. Similarly, when thousands of self-sacrificing citizens join in, a society becomes vibrant. It encourages mutual helpfulness, stimulates pride, brings dignity to work and broadens our mental horizons.

> *The salvation of mankind lies only in making everything the concern of all.*
>
> – Alexander I Solzhenitsyn

We must remember two cardinal truths – greatness emerges out of goodness and democracy never dies suddenly; it gradually becomes defunct through the indifference of its citizens.

> *Ask not what your country can do for you, ask what you can do for your country.*
>
> – John F. Kennedy

For good citizens, patriotism is a way of life. Responsible citizens have a great mission in life. All great leaders in history had their personal agendas totally aligned with the national agendas. There was no hidden agenda.

A free nation needs to remember with gratitude the men who made its freedom possible. A nation that forgets its freedom fighters stands to lose its own freedom.

GOD AND THE SOLDIER

God and the soldier
All men adore
In time of trouble,
And no more;
For when war is over
And all things righted,
God is neglected –
The old soldier slighted.

– Anonymous

Patriotism – Is It Necessary?

The creed of patriotism has met with many critics in its long history. According to Samuel Johnson, "Patriotism is the last refuge of the scoundrel." If treachery is to be camouflaged under the cloak of patriotism, then Mr Johnson is right. But that is not patriotism. If that were patriotism, then the Washingtons, the Lee Kwan Yews and the Lincolns were scoundrels.

Three questions arise:

- *Is patriotism national pride or chauvinism?*

- *Is defense spending a waste of precious resources?*
- *Isn't patriotism outdated in the age of the global village?*

Citizens must realise that every product of the country that carries the label, "Made in ..." also carries the respect and dignity of every citizen of that country. Making the finest product to the best of their ability is true pride in the country. Taking pride in one's own country does not necessarily translate into the attitude: "My country is better than yours". That is a very distorted point of view. Patriotism which involves pulling down other nations, amounts to chauvinism and is criminal.

People argue that in the name of patriotism billions of dollars are spent on armies, money which could have been better used for humanitarian purposes. But so long as there are terrorists and people like Hitler in this world, threatening the respect and dignity of other nations and oppressing humanity, there will always be need for armies to defend the honour of peace-loving nations. No wonder they are called defense forces not attack forces. Would any self-respecting nation greet aggressors like Hitler with bouquets and flowers?

It is said that the world today has become a global village, and territorial boundaries have become meaningless. Are we not forgetting that a nation is much more than barbed wires and gates of steel. Just like a title deed to your house the territorial boundaries of a country have their own sanctity.

Traitors

Traitors who betray their country for a handful of gold are never happy. They end up losing everything.

A young girl used to go out of the fort to draw water everyday. Once, the enemy besieged the fort and appealed to the girl's greed by offering her great wealth and jewels. A bargain was made, and as agreed, the girl unlocked the gates at midnight to let the enemy in. As the first soldier entered, the girl asked him for her reward. He said, "Take your reward" and chopped her arm. The next soldier did the same thing as did the one after him. Soon she lay dead, as dead as the nation she had betrayed.

A French writer once said, *"More men are guilty of treachery through weakness than through a studied design to betray."*

Benedict Arnold was one such traitor. During the American War of Independence he sold military secrets to the British. His countrymen discovered the plot, but Arnold managed to escape to England. However, even in England people did not want to speak to him, or to be seen around him. He was grossly insulted in public places. It is said that some people spat on his face. Wherever he went, his reputation as a traitor followed him. He was always known as "Benedict Arnold, the Traitor".

Freedom is not FREE.

ACTION PLAN

1. Identify and take up a cause that will help improve society. Cause such as -- AIDS or child abuse or forced prostitution.

2. If you don't know where to start join a group such as Rotary, the Lions, Junior Chambers, Round Table, etc.

3. Get politically active so that you can influence the decision-making process in your society.

SELF-EVALUATION SHEET

_____

_____

_____

_____

_____

_____

_____

_____

_____

_____

_____

_____

_____

_____

_____

_____

10

JUSTICE

Truth in Action

There is no crueler tyranny than that which is per-petrated under the shield of law and in the name of justice.

– Charles-Louis de Secondat
Baron de Montesquieu in 1742

*J*ustice and honourable living go hand in hand. Where law and justice do not exist, tyranny prevails.

Mayor La Guardia was once presiding at a New York city night court. The weather was cold and wintry. All of a sudden, a trembling man was brought in and charged with stealing a loaf of bread. When questioned, the man explained that he had to steal in order to feed his starving family. La Guardia declared, "I have to punish you. There can be no exception to the law. I fine you $10." As he gave his verdict, he pulled $10 from his pocket and paid the fine. "Furthermore", he declared, "I am going to fine everyone in this courtroom 50 cents for living in a city where a man has to steal bread in order to eat. Mr Bailiff collects the fines and gives them to the defendant."

In a judicial system, people must be held accountable for their actions and be made to bear their consequences. But at the same time the judicial system must also show compassion in situations that genuinely demand it. Justice should not only be done but also be perceived as having been done. This is not to say that people will be allowed to get away by doing wrong or commit a crime in the expectation that they will be forgiven on compassionate grounds. Many perpetrators take great comfort from the feeling that if caught they have the opportunity to lie and go scot free. The greatest incentive in committing crime is the assurance that one can escape punishment. If crime is overlooked, it encourages the perception that moral wrongdoing is acceptable. Such an attitude would amount to an exploitation of compassion that is built into a genuine understanding of justice. Justice must distinguish between the vicious and the unfortunate.

A state is better governed which has but few laws, and those laws strictly observed...

– Rene Descartes

There is an ancient story. Once Truth and Deceit were travelling together. Truth looked rather starved and was wearing rags. Deceit said, "You seem to be in a pretty bad shape" and Truth replied, "Yes, I am. Nobody respects me or even gives me a job, but they make fun of me." Deceit convinced Truth to follow his way and change his lifestyle for the better. Truth decided to follow Deceit on the promise that he would not say anything against Deceit. Truth decided to follow Deceit not because he felt that it was right but because he was starved. They went to a fine restaurant. Deceit placed the order and they ate some of the finest food. But before they got down to paying the bill, Deceit shouted and called the Manager and said he was waiting for the change from the waiter. The waiter was summoned. He was stunned because he had not taken any money. Deceit shouted at the Manager accusing them to be a bunch of thieves and taking innocent people for a ride. The Manager became concerned about his reputation, refused to accept any money and instead gave out money from his own pocket which was to have been the "change", if what was being said was true. Deceit and Truth heard the Manager shouting at the waiter and threatened to fire him despite his protests. The waiter wondered in his heart if Truth had deserted hard-working souls. Truth felt guilty and said to himself, "My judgement gave away to my hunger." Deceit came out walking tall. Truth could not take anymore and parted company silently.

"There are no principles on empty stomach."

– Mahatma Gandhi

When money talks, truth remains silent. Silence and integrity are two different things. Just because the person is silent does not mean they have integrity. More lies have been told in history by remaining silent when we should have spoken.

A good and faithful judge must strive to determine what is right rather than who is right. *Judicial verdicts may not change hearts but they certainly can prevent people from being heartless.*

The world today needs more justice than charity. Often charity becomes necessary because of injustice.

The moving spirit behind any great cause is the call for justice. *There are times when injustice cannot be prevented but there should never be a time when it cannot be protested.* Bad laws constitute the worst kind of injustice. A law that cannot punish the guilty cannot persuade the citizens to respect and honour its code. A society not only need good laws to restrain bad people but also good people to restrain bad laws.

For some people, it is lack of moral strength that makes them succumb to wrongdoing while others actively seek opportunities to do wrong. Crime is the consequence of ignoring the conditions that breed lawlessness.

What Punishment for a Loaf of Bread

There was a man without a job, who was suffering with abject poverty. He had a family who was starving to death. One cold winter night he could not see his children's misery and hunger. He went to the neighbourhood baker and stole a loaf of bread. He was caught, arrested and convicted. He was sentenced to jail for two years. While in prison, he kept thinking of his famished children. He tried to escape but was caught, and more years were added to his sentence. Then he made second and third attempt which also failed and he ended up serving fifteen years in jail, for only one loaf of bread. When he came out of the prison, he became insensitive. His bitterness towards society reflected in his behaviour.

At the end of the judgement, many times we wonder who won – the best man or the best liar?

Lying under oath is stealing someone's future. Most cases in the courts have a plaintiff and a defendant who give contradictory stories. Sometimes, the contradictions may be a matter of perception but at other times, we know that someone is lying, especially when both parties have something to gain.

Another reason for such lying is misguided loyalties. By-standers not coming forward with truth may not be labelled as purjury but is certainly distortion of justice.

Obstructing the path of justice is like committing treachery against the nation. Where justice is denied, the State becomes an organised conspiracy to oppress its citizen, peace cannot prevail.

Injustice to anyone or anywhere in society is a threat to justice everywhere.

No country can survive where:

- Lawlessness becomes the law
- The guilty go unpunished
- The dishonest are rewarded
- Citizens are indifferent
- Custodians of the law become the biggest lawbreakers.

Law and justice go hand in hand; we cannot have one without the other. *Every time a case is tried, both the law and the judiciary are on trial.* Law is not necessarily the same as justice nor is trial always a true investigation into truth. It may just be a resolution of dispute.

This is a court of law, young man, not a court of justice.

– Oliver Wendell Holmes Jr

Freedom becomes meaningless in the absence of justice. People don't mind harsh laws but they mind the selective handing out of justice.

If a judicial system does not appeal to intelligence – it is bad, if it hurts conscience – it's criminal, if it corrupts character – it is vicious.

In a corrupt society, dual systems are institutionalised. There are official and unofficial procedures for everything. What starts as speed money, ends up as blackmail and extortion and finally leads to the destruction of society.

The Difference Between Partners in Crime and Victims in Crime in a Corrupt Society

If I apply for a license and deprive a more deserving third party by bribing the authorities, I become a partner in crime while the deprived third party becomes a victim.

Let us take a look at a life-and-death situation. If you pick up someone who is bleeding profusely on the street and take him to the hospital, nobody there seems to care. In a corrupt society, if you bribe someone they'll take him on right away. Your principles teach you not to bribe. The question then arises, would you let this person bleed to death or bribe? Put in a situation like this, I will bribe. Legally I just became a criminal, but ethically I saved a life.

Years later, I may be declared innocent. Who cares? I may be dead anyway. I broke the law but I saved a life. The question is, am I a partner in crime or its victim? Majority would agree I am a victim. I feel strongly that most people are honest, they are not partners in crime but in corrupt societies, they become victims of crime.

> *Cooperation is a duty only so long as the government protects your honour. When the government, instead of extending protection, robs you of your honour non-cooperation becomes your duty.*
>
> – Mahatma Gandhi addressed over 50,000 people in Madras on 12th August 1920

Where lawlessness becomes the law of the land, honest citizens become cheats, crooks and dacoits. To do the legal thing, they have to do illegal things.

Law of the Land and Law of Humanity

Many great leaders challenged the judiciary to uphold humanity. Some of the greatest leaders, like the Gandhis and Martin Luther Kings, broke the law of the land. Gandhi broke many colonial laws. Anyone who breaks a law commits a crime, then

Gandhi was one of the biggest criminals in history, for Gandhi held that the law of humanity was way above the law of land.

Take away justice, and what is a state but a large band of robbers.

– St Augustine

Whenever legal rights come into conflict with human rights – the question of fairness and justice need to be re-examined.

Gandhi showed the way by breaking the salt tax law because it hurt the poorest of the poor. The protest had tremendous emotional appeal. When Gandhi made salt at Dandi, he broke the salt law and the hundreds who followed in his footsteps did the same and courted arrest. This act of breaking the law was a protest against the inhumanity of colonial administration. This was a challenge to the judiciary to uphold humanity. Breaking an unjust law and willingly accepting the consequences without running away, showed the highest respect for law. It aroused the collective will of the community against the injustice of the colonial rulers.

Any government that imprisons people unjustly invites citizens' wrath. Arbitrary imposition of pain and injustice ought to be unacceptable to citizens because it kills human dignity and honourable living.

There comes a point in our lives when we are called

upon to take a stand. Gandhi felt morally justified in encouraging others to launch the civil disobedience movement. Without any formal position of power or wealth Gandhi mobilised millions because he devoted his life to the service of his people and the pursuit of justice.

> *Non-cooperation is directed not against men but against measures. It is not directed against the governors, but against the system they administer. The roots of non-cooperation lie not in hatred but in justice...*
>
> – M.K. Gandhi

Any legal system that hurts an honest citizen may be antiquated and in need of re-evaluation. ***Occasionally, standing up for human rights and justice is more important than maintaining peace.***

Sometimes honest citizens are charged as troublemakers because they assert their rights. If standing up for one's rights is a crime then every citizen must strive to be a criminal. When an innocent person is imprisoned or treated unjustly the rest of the society should protest and be prepared to go to prison. If individuals in a society do not support the enforcement of law then no law enforcement agency can help them. Remember those who stood up for the freedom of the people were also called lawbreakers. During the Boston Tea Party for instance, American freedom fighters threw tea into the Boston Harbor. The English colonials called them lawbreakers but they were acting in the best interests of their fellow citizens. They were protesting against the unjust laws imposed upon them.

Extremism in defense of liberty is no vice and moderation in the pursuit of justice is no virtue, Barry Goldwater said.

> *If a government becomes a lawbreaker, it breeds contempt for the law; it invites every man to become a law unto himself.*
>
> – Justice Louis D. Brandeis

Like unenforced laws, unenforced rights can't be said to exist. When injustice and disorder become profitable for the dishonest, they oppose steps to bring justice and order to society. Lack of justice guarantees the downfall of any society.

A weak government is the biggest instrument of oppression and injustice.

William Ewart Gladstone said, *"National injustice is the surest road to national downfall. The question is whether we have to be in agreement with the people to defend them from injustice. The first responsibility and duty of every individual and society is to bring justice."*

Whenever someone stands for justice, he stands for humanity.

Justice can only prevail when the barriers to injustice are eliminated.

We must have a clear sense of judgement about where to build walls and where to build bridges. Justice is the ultimate objective of every civil society. It should be pursued till it is obtained. Justice says all men are created equal and they have the right to life, liberty and the pursuit of happiness. If justice is worth having, it is worth fighting for.

Laws are formed to restraint the passions of men who will not respect reason and justice. An increase in the number of citizens who do not obey good laws is a sign of poor governance. A wise administration knows how to enforce and how to conciliate with dignity.

A man died leaving a large estate. He had two sons and they were fighting about how they should divide the estate. There was a wise man who lived nearby. They approached him to resolve the dispute, with a commitment that whatever he said would be accepted unconditionally. The wise man came up with a formula, that one brother would divide the estate based on his sense of fairness and the other would have the first pick. The dispute was resolved. Justice was done.

The underlying principle behind the old man's decision was that of empathy. He called upon one son to empathise with the other and was successful in resolving the dispute judiciously.

Honourable Living is only possible if justice prevails.

Justice is truth in action.

– Benjamin Disraeli

ACTION PLAN

1. Identify three people in your vicinity who are in need of justice.

   _____

   _____

   _____

2. If they approve your involvement then get the details and take up their calls.

   _____

   _____

   _____

3. Identify three items that need change that would improve the system permanently.

   _____

   _____

   _____

SELF-EVALUATION SHEET

_____

_____

_____

_____

_____

_____

_____

_____

_____

_____

_____

_____

_____

_____

_____

_____

_____

_____

11

HONOUR ABOVE HONOURS

Footprints in Time

A life well-lived is respected the world over. Not only do they make humanity proud but they become jewels of humanity.

"Man of Vision and Courage

SM Lee yesterday received the inaugural Global Integrity Medal from the Kuala Lumpur Society for Transparency and Integrity, the Malaysian

Chapter of the Berlin-based anticorruption coalition group, Transparency International. It said: "The Global Integrity Medal, awarded to Lee Kuan Yew, Senior Minister, the Government of the Republic of Singapore, in recognition of his incredible success, as Prime Minister, in stamping out corruption in Singapore."

In the process, he transformed Singapore, within a remarkably short time, into an island of integrity. It is, therefore, entirely appropriate that he should be the first recipient of this newly-instituted award intended specifically to honour statesmen and women, and other high public officials whose integrity and personal commitment to confront corruption have made a positive and decisive difference to the lives of the people for whose well-being they are responsible.

The story of Singapore as we know it today is the story of the vision, courage and determination of an exceptional man who set out deliberately to create and sustain a society that puts a premium on high standards of public behaviour.

The fact that Singapore occupies so consistently a place of honour at the top table of countries perceived to be the least corrupt in the world according to Transparency International Corruption Perceptions Index, year in and year out, owes much to the solid ethical foundation that he laid those many years ago here in Singapore.

In endorsing this award, the chairman of Transparency International, Dr Peter Eigen, said: "The role of Lee Kuan Yew in fighting corruption in Singapore is well-known and is considered an important model for fighting against corruption."

We are gathered here today to pay tribute to a gifted and distinguished son of the Asia of whom we are all enormously proud because, in both his private and public life, he symbolises, in the fullest measure, the excellency of man.

In honouring him, we also honour integrity, transparency and accountability, the essentials of good governance for which Singapore is so much admired throughout the world. He has made it all so perfectly clear to us that "Integrity is no longer the luxury of the virtuous; it is a business necessity".

It is my privilege, Sir, to present to you the Transparency International Malaysia Global Integrity Medal which has been specially designed by Royal Selangor for just this occasion, as a token of our highest esteem and regard for your outstanding contribution to global integrity."

(Source: *The Sunday Times*, September 17, 2000)

Tunku Abdul Aziz said there was no point in driving a big car, when you pass by a coffee shop and people sitting there point and say: "I gave him money to pay for it"... Now, at 66 years old, he has retired, but is kept even busier fighting corruption as a volunteer... He is the vice-chairman of Transparency International (TI) (Malaysia chapter). In SM Lee's words... Singapore had designed open and transparent systems of government and business to keep people honest... That, together with a vigilant and demanding public, helps to enforce standards in the public, private and people sectors... Singapore was not immune to corruption, collusion and nepotism rampant in many Asian countries. That was so special because "They are no longer as poor and parlous as they were in the 1950s"... He explained it was essential to reward ministers and officials adequately because if it was not done, they would "gravitate" out of the government sector and into the private one.

(Adapted from: *The Sunday Times*: September 17, 2002)

Preparation for Life

John Naber was hoping to compete in the 1973 world championship. The present game was important because the winner would represent the US team. A quick start and he went off and reached the finish line well ahead of the rest. There was a big applause and congratulations were pouring in. When things settled down, the head referee came up to him and said, "I'm afraid you've been disqualified. The turn judge says she didn't see you touch the wall." People over there were shocked. Perhaps, the official had made a mistake. His coach came running and asked, "Do you want to fight

and protest the call? because if the title was important, the official's decision would have to be dis-
puted as it was one's word against the other". The
coach felt Naber could win. The World title was at
stake. Shouldn't America be represented by its fast-
est swimmer? A young man's decision could follow him for the rest of his life and would influence
the kind of person he wanted to be. Whether to
fight the judge's decision or accept was taken in
the blink of an eye. He said to himself, "My parents didn't raise a cheater". He took a decision.
With moist eyes, he told his coach, "I didn't touch
the wall". His friends didn't know what to say. Well,
what can you say to a young man who just won
the race but doesn't get to walk to the award stand.
Friends and strangers wanted him to cry foul and
to claim an injustice and how he had been robbed.
But the truth was that he had broken the rules and
should be held accountable.

The fact that you choose to compete in a game
implies and means clearly that you accept to play
the game by the rules. Football fields have side-
lines and ends-on so that you know when you go
out of boundary. It is important that the better the
athlete, the more those rules ought to be enforced.
*If the rules are bent for the best, what lesson does
that teach the rest?* The lesson for all of us is: why
to be judged by different standards? We are seeing
many examples of unacceptable behaviour being
justified as "everybody is doing it!" "Winning is

everything." It seems to be the motto not only in sports, but in business and in life as well.

In 1976 Olympics at Montreal, he set 4 world records earning 4 gold medals.

Character is not about doing what you have a right to do but doing what's right. Rules offer a sense of fairness and make civilisations possible. Simply following the rules may not make us good people but violating them certainly endangers us. Because whenever we purposefully cheat or even violate the spirit of a rule, we tarnish our greatest trophy – our Honour.

Values provide meaningful guidance for conduct as an employer, employee, parent or as a citizen. Upon these foundations, we build a better society. In life, the question we need to ask ourselves is what is the right thing to do? Not what's expedient, selfish, attention getting.

Naber recalls 25 years later that as he left the stadium, he could hear the winners name for the race he had gone there to win. He felt bad about the race but felt great about himself for the decision he had made. The loss of one race could never have compared with the loss of his self-esteem. Was the race to prove that he was able to swim faster than the other? Was there a lesson for life? What remains a mystery is had Naber been declared a winner and not been disqualified because the turn judge didn't notice, would he have owned up and volunteered to be disqualified. Regardless of the mystery, Naber's decision was certainly honourable and there is a great lesson to be learnt. 25 years later when he became a father, he realised the positive impact of his decision – how could he insist on honesty or respect from his daughter if he had made a different decision when he was her age? How could he teach her that *it is better to be honourable than to be honoured?*

Loving Firmness

In school, I wasn't the brightest kid. In fact, I was the back-bencher troubling the front-benchers. I was the one as I used to enter the class, my teacher used to ask me to go to the corner and stand up as punishment. When I used to ask my teacher, "what have I done to deserve the punishment" and his answer used to be, "nothing as yet, but you will".

Later, in my tenth grade, I cheated in my exams. I was detained. After my mother saw the results, I went to her and apologised. I said, "I'm sorry. I realise my mistake. But, please get me out of the school". She said, "Son, you messed up. You pay for it". I said, "Mom, its embarrassing to sit with a class which was junior to me." She said, "You messed up. You pay for it". I said, "Mom, I apologise. I've learnt my lesson. This way I'm go-ing to lose a year of my life". She said, "You messed up. You pay for it". Then added, "I'd rather see you lose one year of your life than lose your ethics for the rest of your life."

I had to repeat my tenth grade. She was a firm disciplinarian. Today, I am glad that she did what she did. At that time, what she did appeared painful, I did not realise that it was the greatest act of love. She was preparing me to face the world because she realised that the punishments the world would give me would be much harsher. Her words, "You messed up. You pay for it." "I'd rather see you lose one year of your life than lose your ethics for the rest of your life" today echo as the sweetest words in my memory. They gave my life a new direction. Her decision broke my heart but changed my life. She taught me what the world would test me on some day.

I passed my school in first division, fair and square.

It is better to be honourable than to be honoured.

Remember:

Winners
don't do different things.
They
do things differently! ™

– Shiv Khera

Enquire about public and in-house programs from

Qualified Learning Systems

C-6/4, Vasant Vihar, New Delhi – 110 057, India
Tel: 91-11-26148804
Fax: 91-11-26149658, 26142656
E-mail: skhera@del3.vsnl.net.in
Visit us at: www.shivkhera.com

Associate offices:

Singapore: 124,Tanjong Rhu Road, Casuarina Cove,
#06-06
Singapore –436916
Tel: (65) 63481954
Fax: (65) 63424921

USA: 144 North Beverwyck Road # 349,
Lake Hiawatha
NJ 07034, USA
Fax: (973) 3357030

Please send me information on

• The seminar "Blueprint for Success"
• Keynote presentations
• In-house seminars   •
• Public seminars
• Audio, Video
• Books
• Bulk purchase

Name _____ Title _____

Company _____

Address _____

City _____ State _____ Pin Code _____

Telephone (off) _____ Fax _____

E-mail: _____